REMEMBERING
REAGAN

REMEMBERING REAGAN

PETER HANNAFORD

AND

CHARLES D. HOBBS

REGNERY PUBLISHING, INC.
Washington, D.C.

Library of Congress Cataloging-in-Publication Data

Hannaford, Peter.
Remembering Reagan / Peter Hannaford and Charles D.
Hobbs.
p.   cm.
ISBN 0-89526-514-1
1. Reagan, Ronald—Pictorial works.   2. United States—
Politics and government—1981–1989—Pictorial
works.   I. Hannaford, Peter.   II. Hobbs, Charles D.
III. Title.
E877.2H36   1994
973.927—dc20   94-27830
CIP

Published in the United States by
Regnery Publishing, Inc.
An Eagle Publishing Company
422 First St., SE, Suite 300
Washington, DC 20003

Distributed to the trade by
National Book Network
4720-A Boston Way
Lanham, MD 20706

Printed on acid-free paper.

Designed by ARTWORKS DESIGN.

Color separations by Mandarin Offset.

Manufactured in the United States of America by Quebecor/
Kingsport.

10   9   8   7   6   5   4   3   2   1

Books are available in quantity for promotional or premium
use. Write to Director of Special Sales, Regnery Publishing, Inc.,
422 First Street, SE, Suite 300, Washington, DC 20003,
for information on discounts and terms or call (202) 546-5005.

TO

RONALD AND NANCY REAGAN

who have served their country well

ACKNOWLEDGEMENTS

In selecting the photographs for this book we reviewed nearly a quarter of a million of them. This would have been virtually impossible had the collection not been neatly organized by subject matter and chronology, thanks to the skillful work of the Office of Presidential Libraries staff at the National Archives in Washington, D.C., under the able leadership of Douglas Thurman, supervisory archivist. We want to thank especially Mary Finch, archivist, for her cheerful and efficient responses to our many requests for photos.

Ralph Bledsoe, as director of the Reagan Library in Simi Valley, California, helped us in many ways with encouragement and ideas and we are grateful to him.

Our thanks go, too, to the staff of President and Mrs. Reagan in Los Angeles, especially Fred Ryan, chief of staff, Dottie Dellinger, executive assistant to President Reagan, Cathy Goldberg, director of public affairs, and Peggy Grande and Victoria Sullins, assistants to Mr. Ryan.

Last, but certainly not least, we thank our wives, Judy Hobbs and Irene Hannaford, for their constant good humor, thoughtfulness, and loving support.

PETER HANNAFORD
CHARLES D. HOBBS
Washington, D.C.
September 1994

CONTENTS

AUTHORS' PREFACE

THE IDEA FOR THIS BOOK CAME TO ONE OF THE AUTHORS IN 1986, when he saw a snapshot by a White House photographer of President Ronald Reagan watching televised coverage of the *Challenger* space shuttle disaster. The swift destruction of the *Challenger* and its crew, shortly after liftoff and within the view of TV cameras, was played over and over again by the networks to a shocked nation, and Reagan's expression and posture mirrored that shock in a way impossible to put into words.

At that time the White House photographers periodically hung samples of their recent work along the corridors of the West Wing. Even a cursory examination showed that a photographic chronicle of the Reagan presidency, based on photographs taken by White House photographers, could provide insights into both the presidency as a job and Ronald Reagan as president that could not be gleaned from written material alone.

But was such a chronicle feasible? Were there enough photographs of enough events to make a chronicle representative as well as interesting? Would the photographs be accessible, and could they be retrieved in a way that put them clearly and understandably in the context of the events they portrayed?

At first it looked promising: the ubiquitous presence of White House photographers at all events, large and small, meant there would be plenty of raw material to work from, and the status of the photographers as government employees meant their work would be available to the public, subject only to certain limited decisions of the president himself as to how and when they would be made available. We also learned that the White House photo office had been given the task of creating a photographic archive of the Reagan presidency, which meant that some attempt would be made to catalog and facilitate retrieval of the photographs. We felt that everything we needed would be there.

When we set ourselves to the actual task of constructing this book, in late 1991, however, we realized that we had underestimated the effort it would take. We found that the "photographic archives" consisted of well over a million film negatives, representing some four hundred to five hundred snapshots for each day Ronald Reagan was president, including Saturdays and Sundays. The negatives had been developed as tiny contact prints assembled on 8-by-10 inch acetate-covered sheets—twenty to forty prints to a sheet—and stored in large three-ring binders. Each sheet, representing a role of film, had its own number, and each exposure on the sheet was separately numbered. The contents of each binder were identified by sheet numbers and dates. Most of the sheets included the name of the photographer and the date of exposure of the film, and some carried cryptic titles of the covered events, such as "Brandenburg Gate" for Reagan's famous "Tear down this wall, Mr. Gorbachev" speech in Berlin in 1987.

With a few exceptions, such as formal portraits of the cabinet, the pictures were unposed. The White House photographers emulated the technique of their counterparts in the press: rapid-fire exposure of all the frames in one or several rolls of film, with the expectation that a few of the images would capture the essence of the event. Often more than one photographer worked an event, and then they chose complementary angles to put the president in a photographic crossfire.

Our search through the contact prints was tedious and time consuming, but fascinating. Sometimes it was like looking at the sequence of frames in a documentary motion picture. We used two magnifying glasses—a 2X for scanning the print sheets, and a 10X for closer examination and selection of specific prints. Sometimes we were fortunate enough to find an already enlarged 8-by-10 inch glossy print we could use, but for the most part it was a sheet-by-sheet, print-by-print examination of the three-ring binders.

Any chronicle of a contemporary presidency, with or without pictures, is bound to be partial, in both senses of that word. The photographs we chose represent what we considered the most significant themes and events of the Reagan presidency. A president is many things: the leader of the national government, the leader of his political party, the commander-in-chief of the nation's armed forces, the nation's chief diplomat, the chief communicator of national policy, and, sometimes, the voice of the nation's conscience. The president also has a not-so-private personal life as husband, father, friend, and relative. We have tried to portray Ronald Reagan in all these roles, and in the unique combination of formal and informal settings in which an American president is expected to be "at home." Of course, Ronald Reagan was, as he always has been, most at home with his wife Nancy. The love, respect, and trust they felt for each other permeated the Reagan White House, sustained them during bad times, and made the good times just that much better.

Finally, we must admit a personal partiality. Both of us have been associated with Ronald Reagan in a variety of ways for the past quarter century, and we hold him in high regard, both as a political leader and as a man. As governor of California and as president of the United States he governed from principle, with intelligence and good humor and without cynicism or deceit, and he treated his friends and enemies alike with unfailing courtesy and respect.

What did he accomplish? According to both Margaret Thatcher and Aleksandr Solzhenitsyn, he won the Cold War for the West. He presided over the longest period of sustained peacetime economic growth in the nation's history. He rebuilt the nation's defenses and restored the United States to a preeminent position as a world power. He curbed government fiscal and regulatory excesses, not as much as he wanted, but more than any other president in living memory.

Ronald Reagan should and will be remembered for these accomplishments. But perhaps he will be remembered most fondly by his fellow citizens as a man who had the strength and character to handle comfortably the job of president of the United States, and who represented their interests as his own. We hope this book contributes to that memory.

Washington, D.C.
September 1994

"They say a picture is worth a thousand words; but seeing these
photographs of our White House years in one volume has left me thoroughly speechless.
Those White House photographers were around every corner, that's for sure.
They've captured priceless moments which bring back so many wonderful memories."

RONALD REAGAN

REMEMBERING
REAGAN

THE FIRST INAUGURATION

This Administration's objective will be a healthy, vigorous, growing economy.

PRESIDENT RONALD REAGAN, INAUGURAL ADDRESS, JANUARY 20, 1981

O N TUESDAY, JANUARY 20, 1981, Ronald Wilson Reagan became the fortieth president of the United States. The oldest man ever elected president, he was just two weeks shy of his seventieth birthday, but looked much younger.

Powerfully built, photogenic, and an eloquent speaker, Reagan had been a popular public figure for more than four decades. He was also the acknowledged spokesman for a conservative political philosophy that had been gaining support steadily since the 1950s. Although other presidents had espoused parts of that philosophy, Reagan was considered by his followers to be the first true conservative to be elected president in modern times.

Reagan's path to the presidency was an unusual one, encompassing two unexpected careers. Born and reared in small Illinois towns and coming of age during the job-scarce Great Depression of the thirties, he parlayed a sports-announcing job at an Iowa radio station into a successful acting career in motion pictures and television.

Toward the end of that career, in 1964, a nationally televised speech he gave in support of then-presidential candidate Barry Goldwater ignited Republican party interest in making Reagan, himself, a candidate for public office.

He resisted: "I had a good job and a good life and, at fifty-four, the last thing I wanted to do was start a new career." But increasing public enthusiasm for his speeches supporting free enterprise and limited government changed his mind. In

A kiss for good luck

his first try for elected office, in 1966, Reagan soundly—and surprisingly—defeated Democratic incumbent Edmund G. "Pat" Brown, to become governor of California. After two highly successful terms, he narrowly missed becoming the Republican presidential nominee in 1976.

Continuing to build support for himself and his conservative principles in the late seventies, Reagan captured the Republican nomination in 1980 and went on to defeat incumbent President Jimmy Carter, outpolling him by 8.5 million popular votes and garnering 489 of 538 possible electoral votes.

With the nation suffering from double-digit inflation and interest rates (dubbed the "misery index"), an energy shortage, and the indignity of having its Iran embassy staff held hostage by the Ayatollah

Khomeini's fanatic followers, Reagan had been able to focus his campaign message as a simple question to the American people: "Are you better off now than you were four years ago?"

Everything about Inauguration day seemed to promise a change for the better. After a week of bitterly cold weather in the nation's capital, a warming trend set in over the weekend and the temperature climbed to nearly 60° F by the time Reagan took the oath of office on Monday, with his wife Nancy beside him, holding the Reagan family Bible.

For the first time in the nation's history, the ceremony took place on the west steps of the Capitol building, facing the Capitol mall to the Washington Monument, the Lincoln Memorial, and, symbolically, out and beyond to the rest of the troubled nation.

The new president began his Inaugural address under a cloudy sky that suddenly turned to bright sunshine. A *Time* magazine reporter noted the "strange and wonderful event," and how, "Later, a few minutes after he finished speaking, as if on cue from some master lighter backstage,

---

TOP   *The Inaugural parade*

CENTER   *The band from the president's home town* **alma mater,** *Dixon (Illinois) High School, passes in review*

BOTTOM   *Trying out the desk in the Oval Office*

the hole in the clouds shrank, the sky darkened, and Washington grew gray and cold once again."

Reagan's Inaugural address foresaw better times: recovery of the nation's economy and a diminished role for the federal government: "It is time to reawaken this industrial giant, to get government back within its means, and to lighten our punitive tax burden. And these will be our first priorities, and on these principles there will be no compromise."

Following the traditional Capitol lunch with members of Congress, the Reagans made their way in an open limousine down Pennsylvania Avenue to the White House, where they watched the Inaugural parade from a reviewing stand set up on the front lawn. One of the bands in the parade was from the high school in Dixon, Illinois, from which Reagan had graduated fifty-three years before.

That evening the Reagans attended each of the ten Inaugural balls held throughout the city, returning late to the White House and their first night as President and First Lady of the United States.

At the traditional Inaugural luncheon in the United States Capitol building, the new president announces that our hostages have been freed in Tehran

An Inaugural ball

THE HOSTAGES COME HOME

. . . Thirty minutes ago, the planes bearing our prisoners
left Iranian airspace and are free of Iran.

—RONALD REAGAN
INAUGURATION DAY, JANUARY 20, 1981

AN UNPLANNED HIGHLIGHT of Inauguration day was the release by Iran of the Americans who had been held hostage in the United States Embassy in Tehran for more than a year. The new president announced the news during the traditional post-Inauguration luncheon with congressional leaders. Speaking in historic Statuary Hall—the Capitol's original House of Representatives chamber—Reagan declared, "With thanks to Almighty God, I have been given a tag line, the get-off line everyone wants at the end of a toast or speech. Some thirty minutes ago, the planes bearing our prisoners left Iranian airspace and are free of Iran."

Thus ended the 444-day captivity of the embassy staff, one of the most humiliating events in American history. Supporters of Iran's fanatical religious leader, the Ayatollah Khomeini, in a supposedly "popular" outburst against the "Godless" United States, had surrounded the embassy in November 1979 and taken its occupants hostage, demanding that the U.S. turn over the deposed shah of Iran, by then in exile in the United States where he was undergoing cancer treatment. Shortly after the takeover, Khomeini allowed his supporters to release thirteen American women and blacks from the embassy, leaving fifty-two men in captivity, led by *chargé d'affaires* Bruce Laingen.

Then-President Jimmy Carter took retaliatory actions in the United States. He deported illegal Iranian students, froze Iranian assets, and ended oil imports from Iran. These actions had no noticeable effect on Khomeini's refusal to release the remaining hostages. Moreover, Carter's attempt in the spring of 1980 to mount a secret military rescue mission ended in disaster when a navy helicopter crashed in the desert, killing eight American servicemen. Even the shah's death in Egypt in July 1980 brought no hope of the hostages' release.

During the fall election campaign Carter stepped up efforts to negotiate with the Iranians through Algerian and Swiss go-betweens, raising fears among Republicans that he would secure the hostages' release as an "October Surprise" just before the elections. In an effort to defuse the surprise element, Reagan's people began predicting it to reporters during the summer.

But the Carter negotiations proved fruitless: Khomeini held the hostages until Carter left the presidency. When the

The former hostages on the reviewing stand

Reception for former hostages and their families

announcement of the release came, Carter was on his way by limousine to Andrews Air Force Base for the flight home to Plains, Georgia, accompanied by his vice president Walter Mondale. On hearing the news, both men wept.

Reagan, sympathizing with Carter's embarrassment and frustration, invited the former president to use Air Force One to fly to Frankfurt to greet the freed hostages, which Carter did, with Mondale accompanying him. A week later, on January 27, Reagan held a White House reception and public ceremony to honor the freed hostages and the families of the servicemen who had died trying to rescue them. Against a backdrop of American flags, Reagan and the nation honored the men who had endured, on behalf of their fellow Americans, the long and frightening national insult inflicted by the tyrannical Khomeini.

*The president presents a citation to L. Bruce Laingen who had been **chargé d'affaires ad interim** at the embassy in Tehran*

ASSASSINATION ATTEMPT

Whatever happens now, I owe my life to God.

FROM RONALD REAGAN'S DIARY, WRITTEN
AS HE WAS RECOVERING FROM THE SHOOTING

JUST SIXTY DAYS AFTER Reagan's Inauguration—on March 30, 1981—a disturbed young man, John Hinckley, Jr., tried to assassinate him, and very nearly succeeded. Ironically, the Reagans had attended a performance at Ford's Theater just a few days before and the president, looking at the flag-draped box in which Abraham Lincoln had been fatally shot, thought to himself that, even with modern security methods, a determined assassin could probably get close enough to a president to shoot him.

A second irony was that, on March 30, Reagan did not have on the bulletproof vest the Secret Service usually insisted he wear in public, because his public exposure that day was to be very brief.

Reagan gave a luncheon address at the Capital Hilton Hotel that day to a large audience of members of the Construction Trades Council, all of whom had passed through metal detectors as they entered the hall. But, leaving the hall, Reagan had to walk thirty feet from a back entrance of the hotel to his limousine, and it was in those few seconds that he became a target for Hinckley, who was waiting with a gun in a small crowd on the sidewalk.

Reagan waved to the crowd as he walked, then heard popping noises. "What the hell's that?" he asked. Jerry Parr, head of his Secret Service unit, did not answer but grabbed him and literally threw him onto the back seat of the limousine, tumbling in on top of him. Reagan felt a sharp pain in his upper back. He thought Parr's weight had broken a rib. Parr ordered the driver to return to the White House.

Reagan sat up and coughed. Bright red, frothy blood appeared in his hand. Parr looked at it and ordered the driver to go immediately to George Washington University Hospital, a half-mile west of the White House. That quick decision undoubtedly saved the president's life.

At the scene of the shooting, three men were down. Jim Brady, Reagan's press secretary, had been shot in the head; Secret Service Agent Tim McCarthy, in the chest; and Policeman Tom Delehanty, in the neck. Hinckley was quickly overpowered and taken into custody.

Reagan, meanwhile, walked into the hospital emergency room and collapsed. One of Hinckley's bullets had ricocheted off the limousine and entered his body under the left arm. It broke a rib, punctured his left lung, and stopped one inch from his heart. He was bleeding heavily internally. He floated in and out of consciousness as he was given blood transfusions and preparations were made to remove the bullet surgically.

Yet, even in sharp pain and unable to catch his breath, Reagan displayed a self-deprecating humor and the kind of courage Ernest Hemingway once defined as "grace under pressure." Opening his eyes to see Nancy looking down at him, he murmured, "Honey, I forgot to duck."

Leaving the Washington Hilton (Press Secretary James Brady to left and rear of the president)—just before the shooting

And again, when one of the doctors told him they were going to operate, Reagan said, "I hope you're all Republicans." Later, asked by one of the nurses in the recovery room how he felt, he responded with the W.C. Fields line: "All in all, I'd rather be in Philadelphia." Still in critical condition and unable to speak through the tubes and oxygen mask, he wrote a note that read, "Can we rewrite this scene, beginning at the time I left the hotel?"

Considering his age and the severity of his wound, Reagan showed remarkable recuperative powers. Twelve days after the shooting, he returned with Nancy to the White House, wearing a red alpaca sweater over a bulletproof vest. He walked unaided through the Diplomatic entrance to the elevator.

On April 28, less than a month after nearly dying from his wound, Reagan appeared before a joint session of Congress to present his economic recovery package. Receiving "an unbelievable ovation that went on for several minutes," he later joked, "That reception was almost worth getting shot for."

A get-well card from the staff

Back at the White House (April 11, 1981)

25

REVIVING THE ECONOMY

. . . this recovery was created by the incentives of tax rate reductions, which shifted resources away from government back to American producers, savers, and investors.

—RONALD REAGAN
MESSAGE TO CONGRESS, MARCH 19, 1984

RONALD REAGAN'S HIGHEST domestic priority in his first year as president was to revive the economy. During the election campaign he had emphasized the need to change economic and tax policies sharply and, once in office, he moved quickly to mobilize the resources of the federal government to carry out his campaign proposals.

The situation warranted radical change. At the beginning of 1981 the economy was in its worst shape in forty years: inflation was running 13.5 percent annually, unemployment was above 7 percent and rising, the banks' prime lending rate was

Returning to Capitol Hill for the joint session speech (April 28, 1981)

an incredible 21.5 percent, and real wages of American workers had fallen 9 percent in the preceding two years. In 1979, then-President Jimmy Carter spoke of a national "malaise," reflecting the widespread belief among political observers that the nation had entered an "era of limits" and even, perhaps, a course of slow but permanent economic decline.

Reagan disagreed: "I saw no national malaise. I found nothing wrong with the American people." Instead, he diagnosed the economic problem as caused primarily by excessive taxation and federal government spending, exacerbated by inflation-fueling overexpansion of the nation's money supply and overregulation of business which, in turn, discouraged investment and reduced productivity. His

answer: cut taxes, reduce the growth rate of government spending, eliminate growth-inhibiting regulations, and stabilize the money supply.

In his first week in office, Reagan held three cabinet meetings to discuss his plan for economic recovery. He devoted his first meeting with congressional leaders to the same subject. He also signed orders deregulating petroleum prices and establishing a task force on regulatory reform to be chaired by Vice President George Bush.

On February 18, only a month in office, Reagan delivered his proposed economic recovery program to Congress, summarizing the four major elements as:

A budget reform plan to cut the rate of growth in federal spending;

A series of proposals to reduce personal income tax rates by 10 percent a year over three years and to create jobs by accelerating depreciation for business investment in plant and equipment;

A far-reaching program of regulatory relief;

And, in cooperation with the Federal Reserve Board, a new commitment to a monetary policy that will restore a stable currency and healthy financial markets.

Congressional reception to the plan was cool, particularly in the Democrat-controlled House of Representatives, but also among the more senior members of the Republican-controlled Senate. They were concerned that tax reduction would mean lost revenues and a large deficit. Reagan believed that an income tax rate cut would rekindle the economy and produce higher revenues, as previous cuts had done in the Harding and Kennedy administrations.

The congressional debate had just begun to percolate when John Hinckley's bullet put Reagan on the sidelines for nearly a month. Although he rejoined the debate on April 28, with a powerful and enthusiastically received address to a joint session of Congress, congressional resistance remained strong to the proposed 30 percent income tax cut. Even some of Reagan's key advisors began to have fears about its effect on the federal budget, given the reluctance of Congress to control spending. In late May, Reagan acquiesced reluctantly to reducing the tax cut from 30 percent to 23 percent.

In an attempt to derail the Reagan plan, the Democratic leadership proposed its own "tax relief" plan, which Reagan compared to his own in a nationally televised speech on July 27. "The plain truth is, our choice is not between two plans to reduce taxes; it's between a tax cut or a tax increase." He spent the whole of July 28 lobbying Congress by phone, in anticipation of a vote the following day.

Polls showed overwhelming public support for his program, and the members of Congress he talked with admitted being flooded with constituent calls telling them to vote for the Reagan tax cut. That night he wrote in his diary, "Tomorrow is the day, and it's too close to call. But there is no doubt the people are with us."

Drafting his speech to Congress (April 1981)

Reagan makes a point about taxes in his televised speech (July 1981)

The vote was overwhelming in the Senate: 89 for, 11 against. In the House it was much closer, 238 to 195—the margin of difference being the "ayes" of some forty "boll weevils," Southern Democrats from districts Reagan had carried strongly in the 1980 election.

The tax cuts had exactly the effects Reagan had anticipated: they triggered a ninety-two-month period of economic growth, from November 1982 to July 1990. From trough to peak, the Gross

National Product (GNP) grew 32 percent, or 4.2 percent a year. Federal tax receipts doubled between 1980 and 1990, while remaining unchanged as a percentage of GNP. Annual disposable personal income, per capita, rose in constant dollars (that is, adjusted for inflation) from $9,722 in 1980 to $11,973 in 1990. Inflation tumbled, from the double-digit numbers Reagan inherited in 1981 to an average annual rate of less than 4 percent between 1982 and 1989. Interest rates also fell sharply: by

1987 the prime lending rate was at 8.2 percent. Unemployment rose through 1981, peaked at 9.7 in 1982, then declined steadily to 5.3 in 1989.

Despite their beneficial effects on the economy and government revenues, the tax cuts did not solve the deficit problem because Congress refused to limit the growth of federal spending. While tax receipts were doubling, spending was more than doubling. During this period of rapid GNP growth, congressionally mandated spending actually grew as a percentage of GNP, from 22.1 percent in 1980 to 24.3 percent in 1983, and close to 24 percent through 1986. In 1983, 1985, and 1986, the congressional budget required that Reagan spend at least 5 percent more of GNP than the federal government received in revenues. This spending binge produced a staggering $1.3 trillion in total deficits over the eight years Reagan was in office.

Chafing at his inability to rein in the deficit-spending habits of Congress,

October 20, 1987, reviewing with advisors the developments in financial markets following the huge fluctuations the day before (l. to r.: Federal Reserve Chairman Alan Greenspan, Chief of Staff Howard Baker, Reagan, Treasury Secretary James Baker)

Reagan proposed structural spending restraints: a constitutional amendment to require a balanced budget, along with line-item veto authority that would allow the president to cut unnecessary spending. But both proposals were repeatedly rejected by Congress. Thus Reagan, the president who masterminded one of the strongest and most persistent eras of prosperity in the nation's history, also presided over the greatest accumulation of federal debt in history.

Trained in economics himself, Reagan surrounded himself with distinguished conservative economists. He created a President's Economic Policy Advisory Board, chaired by banker Walter Wriston, and including Nobel Laureate Milton Friedman, ex-Federal Reserve Board Chairman Arthur Burns, and Alan Greenspan, later to become chairman of the Federal Reserve Board.

In addition to the 1981 tax cuts, Reagan persuaded Congress to index income tax brackets for inflation, beginning in 1985, thereby eliminating "bracket creep," the imposition of ever-higher tax rates based on purely inflationary income increases. Later, in 1986, Reagan engineered a major overhaul of the income tax law, compressing many income tax brackets into just three and effectively eliminating federal income taxes for low-income families.

Rounding up votes by telephone (July 1981)

The continuing problem of federal deficits cast a shadow on the prosperity of the Reagan era and was blamed for every fluctuation in the economy, including, for example, the largest one-day price decline experienced in seventy years by the stock market on October 19, 1987. Overall, however, Reagan's tax-cutting and regulatory relief policies were vindicated by the strong economic recovery they produced and sustained throughout the decade.

The president meets with his Economic Policy Advisory Board, including Rep. Jack Kemp, Rita R. Campbell, Alan Greenspan, Donald Regan, Milton Friedman, and George Shultz (September 10, 1981)

Signing the tax reform bill, October 1986

G-7, THE ECONOMIC SUMMIT CONFERENCES

*. . . the economic summits . . . were, by and large,
productive forums for frank discussions of economic issues,
which in today's world extend more and more across
international boundaries.*

FROM *AN AMERICAN LIFE* BY RONALD REAGAN

ONE OF THE NEW PRESIDENT'S first forays into international politics was the 1981 Group of Seven ("G-7") economic summit conference, held in July at the historic Montebello resort in Quebec, Canada. Reagan thought of himself as "the new boy in school" at this sixth annual meeting of the leaders of the world's seven most important industrialized nations.

He immediately found a kindred spirit in Margaret Thatcher, the British prime minister, who had impressed him from their first meeting in 1975. While the others were friendly, he suspected that several of them, particularly Helmut Schmidt of West Germany, François Mitterand of France, and Pierre Trudeau of Canada, "didn't think much" of his tax-cutting and deregulation ideas.

Reagan, however, was surprised and

The Ottawa summit, 1981

delighted by the informal congeniality of the group, which he attributed to Margaret Thatcher's influence. All called one another by their first names, a practice Reagan found refreshing. At his first chance to speak, he said, "My name's Ron. . . ."

At the next G-7 meeting, in May 1, 1982, at Versailles, he accepted invitations to address the British and West German parliaments on the subject of nuclear war and weapons. Seeking to allay European fears that "were being fired up by demagogues depicting me as a shoot-from-the-hip cowboy aching to pull out my nuclear six-shooter and bring on doomsday," Reagan took the position that "Our military strength is a prerequisite to peace." He also predicted the imminent demise of communism, reminding his listeners that "The decay of the Soviet experiment should come as no surprise to us. . . . Of all the millions of refugees we've seen in the modern world, their flight is always from, not toward the communist world."

By the time Reagan hosted the 1983

OPPOSITE   The Reagans with Emperor Hirohito at the Tokyo summit dinner, 1986

meeting in Williamsburg, Virginia, his economic recovery program was showing positive results, while most of the other G-7 nations were still mired in recession. The skepticism toward his policies that he had felt in Quebec was gone. As they sat down to dinner the first night, Helmut Kohl, who had replaced Schmidt as chancellor of West Germany, spoke for the group. "Tell us," he said, "about the American miracle."

Colonial Williamsburg itself was the ideal American location for the meeting. A privately financed, faithful restoration of the capital of the Virginia Colony in the 1770s, it captures in its structures and

exhibits and in the work of its resident scholars and artisans, the intellectual and cultural spirit of the American Revolution. The G-7 leaders absorbed American history, along with Reagan's prescriptions for economic recovery.

At succeeding summits, in London in 1984 and Bonn in 1985, Reagan was gratified to find that several of the G-7 nations had adopted his economic prescriptions with success. He also found the company even more congenial, as Brian Mulroney replaced Trudeau as prime minister of Canada, and Yasuhiro Nakasone replaced Suzuki as prime minister of Japan. Reagan and Mitterand, a socialist, seldom agreed on policy matters, but the informal atmosphere of the G-7 meetings produced open discussions of differences that led to closer cooperation among the group.

These fruitful discussions continued to characterize later summits, in Tokyo in 1986 and Venice in 1987, where terrorism and reductions in short- and intermediate-range nuclear weapons were primary subjects.

The economic summits seemed least productive to Reagan in the area of trade: "At all eight of the economic summits I attended, I tried to preach the virtues of free trade. In principle, the other leaders expressed a similar view, and denounced the trade barriers of other nations. But the plain truth was that all of us were protectionist to some extent."

Informal dinner at the Venice summit, 1987

THE MIDDLE EAST

*Our involvement in the search for Mideast peace is not a
matter of preference; it's a moral imperative.*

RONALD REAGAN
ADDRESS TO THE NATION, SEPTEMBER 1, 1982

*Welcoming ceremony for President Anwar
Sadat, August 1981*

AMONG THE TOUGHEST
foreign policy problems President
Reagan faced were those related to the
Middle East where, as he put it, "Hate has
roots reaching back to the dawn of
history." Iran's release of the American
Embassy hostages on Inauguration day,
1981, was an event to celebrate, but it was
also a sobering reminder of the difficulties
facing any president in dealing with that
region.

In the first year-and-a-half of the
Reagan administration there was concern
whether Israel would adhere to its treaty
with Egypt, negotiated at Camp David in
1978 by then-President Jimmy Carter.

The Camp David Accords called for
Egypt to recognize the existence of Israel
as a sovereign state, in return for Israel's
promise to return the Sinai peninsula
(occupied since the Six Day War in 1967)
to Egypt, and to grant autonomy to
Palestinians living in the Gaza Strip and
the West Bank of the Jordan River and the
Dead Sea. The return of the Sinai was
scheduled for April 1982.

Reagan met with the first of the major
players in the Middle East drama,
President Anwar Sadat of Egypt, in August
1981. It had been Sadat who, four years
earlier, had flown to Jerusalem as a
gesture of peace, thawing the icy hostility
between Israel and Egypt and setting the
stage for the Camp David Accords. Sadat's
recognition of Israel had infuriated most of
the Arab world, and Egypt was suspended
from the Arab league for ten years.

In two days of meetings, Reagan and
Sadat struck up a close friendship. Reagan
wrote that "Sadat is a very likable man,
with both a sense of humor and a sense of
dignity." In addition to the Arab-Israeli

dispute, they discussed Egypt's problems
with Libya and Iran and with the
fundamentalist Muslim terrorists
sponsored and supported by Muammar
Qadaffi and the Ayatollah Khomeini. As a
result of his efforts to make peace with
Israel, Sadat knew that he had become the
terrorists' prime target.

Two weeks later, Israel's prime minister
and negotiator of the Camp David
accords, Menachem Begin, arrived in
Washington, mainly to lobby Reagan and
Congress against a proposed sale of
American AWACS (Airborne Warning and
Control Systems) aircraft to Saudi Arabia.

Begin contended that these flying

command posts, which could launch and
control both offensive and defensive
weapons, might tip the region's balance of
power against Israel. Reagan disagreed,
believing that the AWACS sale would have
the positive effect of bringing the Saudis,
ostensibly less hostile than their neighbors,
more actively into the peace process. The
Senate, by a narrow margin, refused to
block the AWACS sale to the Saudis, and
it went ahead. Reagan described his own
lobbying efforts against those of Begin as
"one of the toughest battles of my eight
years in Washington."

On October 6, 1981, less than two
months after he had met with Reagan,
Sadat was assassinated by Muslim
fundamentalists. The news hit the Reagans
"like a locomotive . . . suddenly this
great, kind man, filled with warmth and
humor, was gone; it was an enormous
tragedy for the world and a terrible and
painful personal loss for us."

Reagan, horrified, watched Qadaffi
"gloat on television over Sadat's death
while Libyans danced in the streets."
Meeting with his National Security
Council, Reagan considered how to
respond, settling reluctantly at that time
for only a back-channel diplomatic
communication to Qadaffi that terrorism
against Americans would be considered an
act of war.

Sadat was replaced by his vice
president, Hosni Mubarak, who paid a
state visit to Reagan the following
February. Mubarak emphasized Egypt's
friendship for the United States. In return,
Reagan doubled a previously negotiated
$200 million grant to Egypt so that
Mubarak "would have something to take
home."

With Sadat and Vice President Bush, the Oval Office

With Prime Minister Begin, the Oval Office

NSC meets following Sadat assassination, October 1981 (clockwise: CIA Director William Casey, Defense Secretary Caspar Weinberger, Bush, Reagan, Secretary of State Alexander Haig, Counsellor Edwin Meese, White House Chief of Staff James Baker)

Meanwhile, Lebanon, long a base for Palestine Liberation Organization (PLO) terrorist attacks against Israel, became a hotter regional "hot spot" than before as the USSR supplied weapons to Syria and PLO forces along the Israeli border. Within Israel, Begin was under intense pressure to dump the Camp David Accords and to refuse to turn over the Sinai to Egypt. Resisting these pressures, Begin and Mubarak completed the transfer on April 25, 1982.

Reagan telephoned his congratulations to both men. He later recalled, "My heart went out especially to Begin. I had many difficulties with him when I was president, but he was an Israeli patriot devoted, above all, to the survival of his country."

With President Mubarak, February 1982

THE SUPREME COURT

The only litmus test I wanted . . . was the assurance of a judge's honesty and judicial integrity. . . . I wanted judges who would interpret the Constitution, not try to rewrite it.

—RONALD REAGAN, *AN AMERICAN LIFE*

No PRESIDENT SINCE Franklin Roosevelt has had a greater impact on the composition and direction of the federal courts than Ronald Reagan. He appointed 371 federal judges—nearly half the federal judiciary, including three new Supreme Court Justices—and he elevated another to the position of Chief Justice. When George Bush succeeded Reagan in the Oval Office, his first two judicial appointees were men who had been considered favorably for nomination by the Reagan administration.

Reagan's impact went far beyond the number of judicial appointments. His appointees reversed a forty-year liberal drift of the courts epitomized by the Supreme Court of the fifties and sixties under Chief Justice Earl Warren. Warren had been appointed by President Dwight Eisenhower, who later said that appointing Warren had been his "biggest mistake as president."

The Warren Court greatly expanded the power of the federal government to require, permit, or proscribe activities that had, until then, been left to state or local governments or individual judgment. Examples included *Abington Township* v. *Schempp* (1963), which banned prayer in public schools, and *Griswold* v. *Connecticut* (1964), which declared unconstitutional a state law banning contraceptives.

In criminal matters, the Warren Court leaned heavily in favor of the rights of the accused, as in *Mapp* v. *Ohio* (1961), which extended to state courts a federal court rule excluding illegally obtained evidence, *Sheppard* v. *Maxwell* (1966), which overturned a murder conviction because of prejudicial pretrial publicity, and *Miranda* v. *Arizona* (1966), which overturned a rape conviction on grounds that the convicted rapist had not been warned properly of his right to avoid self-incrimination.

With Court nominee Sandra Day O'Connor

With Court nominee Antonin Scalia, Chief Justice nominee Rehnquist, and retiring Chief Justice Burger

Even after Warren's retirement the Court continued to usurp what had previously been state authority under the Tenth Amendment to the Constitution. *Swann v. Charlotte-Mecklenburg Board of Education* mandated school busing as a means of ending segregation, *Furman v. Georgia* (1972) declared state capital punishment laws invalid as "cruel and unusual punishment," and *Roe v. Wade* (1973) invalidated state laws against abortion.

One of Reagan's first acts as president was to ask Ed Meese, then counsellor to the president, and Attorney General William French Smith to establish a system for selecting potential judges based on judicial and personal qualifications, not politics. According to Reagan, "I didn't want politics to play any part in the selection. I wanted the *best* man or woman for the job."

Reagan also asked Smith and Meese to develop a list of qualified women candidates for him to consider for his first Supreme Court appointment. The opportunity came quickly. When Justice Potter Stewart retired in the summer of 1981, Reagan nominated Judge Sandra Day O'Connor of Arizona to be the first woman ever to serve on the Supreme

Court. She easily won Senate confirmation. Reagan later wrote, "I had no doubt she was the right woman for the job . . . she turned out to be everything I hoped for." He had to wait five years for his next opportunity. In mid-1986, Chief Justice Warren Burger retired to head the Bicentennial of the Constitution Commission. Again Reagan broke precedent, this time by nominating a sitting associate justice, William Rehnquist, to become Chief Justice.

Rehnquist was acknowledged throughout the legal professional as a fine scholar, and his fourteen-year record on the Court convinced Reagan that, as Chief Justice, he would lead the Court in exercising the kind of judicial restraint Reagan favored—interpreting the Constitution rather than rewriting it.

To fill Rehnquist's Associate Justice seat, Reagan chose another noted legal scholar and advocate of judicial restraint, Antonin Scalia, a judge on the Federal Court of Appeals for the District of Columbia. Both men were confirmed by the Senate, but not before Rehnquist was subjected to intense questioning and ideological attack by Democrats on the Senate Judiciary Committee.

In 1987, Justice Lewis Powell retired, and Reagan nominated another judge from the Federal Court of Appeals for the District of Columbia (and a well-known legal scholar), Robert Bork. Widely published and outspoken in his support of judicial restraint, Judge Bork was anathema to liberal Democrats, not only because of his philosophy, but also because, as solicitor general in the Justice Department in 1983, he had, on instructions from President Richard Nixon, fired Watergate Special Prosecutor Archibald Cox.

At this time, the Democrats were again in control of the Senate. Even before the committee began its hearings, one of its members—Edward Kennedy—claimed that, with Bork on the Court, "women would be forced into back-alley operations, blacks would sit at segregated lunch counters, rogue police would break down citizens' doors in midnight raids, school children would not be taught about evolution, writers and authors would be censored at the whim of government . . ." This wild hyperbole set the tone for the committee hearings in which, as Meese put it, Judge Bork was "demonized" for his judicial philosophy while his

The Court in 1985, before the retirement of Chief Justice Warren E. Burger (on Reagan's right). At this time, Justice Sandra Day O'Connor was Reagan's only appointee. Justice William H. Rehnquist (on O'Connor's left) would later replace Burger as chief justice.

unassailable professional qualifications were mainly ignored. Both the committee and the full Senate rejected Bork, dealing Reagan a rare defeat in his continuing struggle with congressional liberals.

Despite the loss, Reagan persisted in his quest for judges without political agendas, nominating Californian Anthony Kennedy to fill the Powell seat. Kennedy, a former professor of constitutional law at the University of the Pacific's McGeorge Law School, had spent twelve years on the Federal Ninth Circuit Court of Appeals, a position for which then-California Governor Reagan had recommended him in 1974. Perhaps because the Senate Judiciary Committee had worn itself out on Judge Bork, or because Judge Kennedy presented himself in a less confrontational manner, the hearings were almost perfunctory, leading to a 97-0 Senate vote of confirmation.

With Justice Kennedy's confirmation, Reagan had achieved a major redirection of the Supreme Court. His three new appointees were young enough to look forward to many years on the Court. George Bush's first two appointees—David Souter and Clarence Thomas—were also proponents of judicial restraint.

In the opinion of at least some legal experts, Reagan had raised the overall quality of the entire federal judiciary. Professor Sheldon Goldman of the University of Massachusetts wrote that "assuming that the ABA [American Bar Association] ratings are a reasonably accurate assessment of the credentials of appointees, the [Reagan] second term appointments, on the whole, may turn out to be the most professionally qualified group of appointees over the last two decades."

For Reagan, however, the most important thing was that a candidate's judicial philosophy be grounded in the Constitution and common sense. His own judicial philosophy is perhaps best illustrated by two comments he made during his presidency:

You know, Senator Kennedy was at a dinner recently, the ninetieth birthday party for former Governor and Ambassador Averell Harriman. Teddy Kennedy said that Averell's age was only half as old as Ronald Reagan's ideas. And you know, he's absolutely right. The Constitution is almost two hundred years old, and that's where I get my ideas.

and

Sometimes, I can't help but feel the First Amendment is being turned on its head . . . ask yourselves: Can it really be true that the First Amendment can permit Nazis and Ku Klux Klansmen to march on public property, advocate the extermination of people of the Jewish faith and the subjugation of blacks, while the same amendment forbids our children from saying a prayer in school?

RAWHIDE AND RAINBOW*

Nancy, in front of all your friends here today, let me say, thank you for all you do. Thank you for your love. And thank you for just being you.

—RONALD REAGAN, REMARKS AT A LUNCHEON HONORING
MRS. REAGAN, NEW ORLEANS, AUGUST 15, 1988

E ARLY IN THE FIRST TERM, Librarian of Congress Daniel Boorstin encouraged both Ronald and Nancy Reagan to keep personal diaries of their lives in the White House. He said, "We have never had a presidential couple like the two of you, and that alone is an important historical fact. The love and devotion you show to each other isn't seen much . . . these days."

The numerous unposed snapshots of the Reagans together in the White House confirm Boorstin's view: their caring attention to one another is always evident. Both chose the same words to express the importance of the other: "My life didn't really begin until I met Ronnie," and "I think my life really began when I met Nancy."

The closeness and constancy of their marriage inspired confidence in the public, and their shared sense of responsibility spawned an atmosphere of orderliness and stability in the Reagan White House. "In this administration the trains run on time," was a favorite expression among staff members, reflecting the certainty that a schedule made was a schedule kept.

Reflecting on the importance of Nancy to his performance as president, Reagan wrote: "[F]rankly, I'm not sure a man could be a good president without a wife who is willing to express her opinions with the frankness that grows out of a solid marriage. In a good marriage, husband and wife are best friends: if you can't trust your wife to be honest with you, whom can you trust? Nancy was my best friend, and I wanted to know what she thought."

* The Secret Service Communications designations
for the president and Mrs. Reagan

In a typical workday at the White House, the Reagans rarely saw each other between breakfast and late afternoon, except at ceremonies requiring the presence of both. Following breakfast in the second-floor family quarters, Reagan would go to the Oval Office in the West Wing, where he would spend the working day, lunching, alone or with staff. Nancy worked in the family quarters or in the East Wing, where her staff was housed. Both scheduled a time each day to exercise in the exercise room in the family quarters: Nancy in the morning and the president in the early evening.

State dinners were held about once a month in the formal first-floor dining room. On other nights, if family members or guests were present, the Reagans ate in the second-floor family dining room. If they were alone, they often ate from small portable tables in Reagan's study as they watched the evening news. Although they usually found it a pleasant duty to attend state dinners and evening events held for the president, their favorite evenings were the quiet ones at home, when they could relax, talk, and read. On such evenings they asked the White House usher to hold all except emergency calls, and they

usually retired by ten o'clock.

Was theirs a marriage made in heaven? Nancy thought it had more to do with earthly effort. "If our marriage has been successful, it's because Ronnie and I have worked very hard at it. Maybe we tried extra hard because Ronnie had been divorced, and he didn't want to go through *that* again. Both my parents had been divorced, so I, too, had some idea of what that meant."

Reagan, in a more romantic vein, dedicated his autobiography: "To Nancy. She will always be my First Lady. I cannot imagine life without her."

THE CABINET

*Set clear goals and appoint good people to help you
achieve them. As long as they are doing what you have in
mind, don't interfere, but if someone drops the ball,
intervene and make a change.*

—RONALD REAGAN, *AN AMERICAN LIFE*

AS GOVERNOR OF California, Ronald Reagan streamlined the cabinet system and it worked effectively for him for eight years. At the White House he set out to do the same, managing the executive branch of the federal government through a strong cabinet of people chosen for their professional credentials.

Although he generally favored a business management approach to government (and often called on business

The first Reagan cabinet, February 4, 1981 (left to right, seated): Secretary of State Alexander Haig, President Ronald Reagan, Vice President George Bush, Secretary of Defense Caspar Weinberger. Standing: Secretary of Labor Raymond Donovan, Secretary of the Treasury Donald Regan, Secretary of Education Terrel Bell, Director of the Office of Management and Budget David Stockman, Secretary of Transportation Drew Lewis, Secretary of Housing and Urban Development Sam Pierce, Attorney General William French Smith, Secretary of the Interior James Watt, U.S. Representative to the United Nations, Ambassador Jeane Kirkpatrick, Counsellor to the President Edwin Meese III, Secretary of Energy James Edwards, Secretary of Commerce Malcolm Baldrige, U.S. Trade Representative William Brock, Secretary of Health and Human Services Richard Schweicker, Secretary of Agriculture John Block, Director of Central Intelligence William Casey

leaders for advice), Reagan was keenly aware of the difference between his position and theirs. "Some people have suggested that . . . my cabinet meetings resembled the meetings of a corporation's board of directors. I suppose that's true, but there was one difference: We never took a vote . . . [W]hen the discussion was over, it was up to me and me alone to make the decision."

The cabinet at the beginning of the second term, January 20, 1985 (left to right, front row): Regan (Treasury), Bush, Reagan, Secretary of State George Shultz, Weinberger; (second row) Bell (Education), Kirkpatrick (UN), Stockman (OMB), Smith (Attorney General), Secretary of Transportation Elizabeth H. Dole, Secretary of the Interior Donald P. Hodel, Secretary of Health and Human Services Margaret Heckler; (third row) Block (Agriculture), Donovan (Labor), Baldrige (Commerce), Pierce (Housing & Urban Development) Secretary of the Interior William P. Clark, Casey (CIA), Meese (Counsellor to the President), Brock (USTR)

Initially, Reagan installed an eighteen-member cabinet, including the secretaries of state, treasury, defense, interior, agriculture, commerce, labor, health and human services, transportation, housing and urban development, energy, and education; the attorney general; the counsellor to the president; the director of the Office of Management and Budget; the director of central intelligence; the permanent U.S. representative to the United Nations; and the U.S. trade representative. In his second term, he added the White House chief of staff and the chairman of the Council of Economic Advisors, but left vacant the position of counsellor to the president when he appointed Ed Meese as attorney general.

The large size of the cabinet, coupled with Reagan's desire to have all major issues pass through it, led him to adopt Meese's recommendation to create "cabinet councils," smaller groups of cabinet members that addressed specific issue areas of multidepartment (but less than full cabinet) interest. The model for the cabinet councils was the National Security Council, established by law in 1947, with the president as chairman, and

the vice president, secretary of state, and secretary of defense as its other members (the chairman of the Joint Chiefs of Staff and the director of central intelligence serve as formal advisors). The NSC addressed foreign policy and defense issues vital to national security. Many of these were classified and therefore not suitable to open consideration by the full cabinet.

In his first term, Reagan created seven cabinet councils (in addition to the NSC) on such aspects of national policy as economic affairs, natural resources, commerce, and trade. Discussion meetings were chaired by designated cabinet members; decision meetings by the president. White House staff members served as executive directors of the councils. The frequency of cabinet council meetings and the number of cabinet members attending varied widely, with the Economic Policy Council being the most active. In the first year, 112 cabinet council meetings were held. The number diminished in succeeding years and at the beginning of Reagan's second term, the seven nonstatutory cabinet councils were reduced to two: the Domestic Policy Council, chaired by the attorney general,

and the Economic Policy Council, chaired by the secretary of the Treasury. Working groups were created by both councils to discuss specific issues and present options for action to the councils. The system, in both the first and second terms, widened the scope of policy discussions and improved coordination among the cabinet departments and between them and the White House.

Usually, cabinet meetings were held each week when the president was not traveling and were limited to an hour and to one or two issues. Typically, Reagan made decisions on the spot, following open discussion of cabinet council recommendations. At cabinet meetings there was a loosely defined pecking order among the members, established by their positions at the cabinet table. These positions reflected the statutory ages of the respective departments and agencies.

The president sat at the middle of one side of the cabinet table, in a chair with a slightly higher back than those of the other cabinet chairs. The vice president sat directly opposite him. The president was flanked by the secretaries of state and defense, representing the two oldest departments. The vice president was flanked by the attorney general and the secretary of the Treasury. The other members were distributed around the oblate table. On the top of each cabinet chair back was a small brass plate designating the official who was to sit there. Senior White House staff members and department staff members brought in for technical information, occupied chairs behind the cabinet members.

Despite the formality of the setting, Reagan put the members in a relaxed mood to generate lively discussion. The only taboo subject was politics *per se*: "I wanted to hear all sides of the issue, but there was one thing I didn't want to hear—the 'political ramifications' of my choices."

Although the composition of the cabinet changed as the years passed, long-term members helped Reagan set a consistent tone and policy framework for its deliberations. Among these were Caspar Weinberger, secretary of defense for almost seven years, who oversaw the restoration of the nation's military security; George Shultz, secretary of state from mid-1982 to the end of the Reagan administration, who shepherded the complex negotiations and summit meetings with the Soviet Union that led to the end of the Cold War; Ed Meese, counsellor to the president in the first term and attorney general through most of the second, who took the lead in domestic policy and management issues; and Donald Regan, first as secretary of the Treasury and later as chief of staff, who was the dominant voice in economic and tax issues.

ABOVE **President Reagan introduces Frank Carlucci as Caspar Weinberger's replacement as secretary of defense, November 5, 1987**

BELOW **Secretary of Agriculture Richard Lyng briefs President Reagan and Vice President Bush on the drought in the West, June 17, 1988**

The cabinet on July 1, 1987 (left to right): Weinberger (defense), Secretary of the Treasury James Baker, Secretary of Education William Bennett, Shultz (State), Secretary of Energy John Herrington, Meese (Attorney General), U.S. Trade Representative Clayton Yeutter, Dole (Transportation), Director of OMB James Miller, Chief of Staff Howard Baker, Baldrige (Commerce), Hodel (Interior), Brock (Secretary of Labor), Secretary of Agricultural Richard Lyng, Secretary of Health and Human Services Otis Bowen, Pierce (HUD), Reagan, Bush

The last cabinet, January 11, 1989 (left to right, front row): Secretary of Defense Frank Carlucci, Shultz (State), Reagan, Bush, Secretary of the Treasury Nicholas Brady, Attorney General Richard Thornburgh; (second row) Secretary of Commerce William Verity, Secretary of Labor Ann McLaughlin, Hodel (Interior), Lyng (Agriculture), Bowen (HHS), Pierce (HUD); (third row) Secretary of Transportation James Burnley, Herrington (Energy), Secretary of Education Lauros Cavazos, Chief of Staff Kenneth Duberstein, Director of OMB Joseph Wright, Ambassador to the UN Vernon Walters, Yeutter (USTR), Chairman of the Council of Economic Advisors Beryl Sprinkel

THE AIR TRAFFIC CONTROLLERS GO ON STRIKE

I believe in collective bargaining in the private sector. I do not believe in it for the public sector because I do not believe that public employees can be allowed to strike. Public employees are striking against the people and the people are the highest source of power—other than the Lord Himself—that the government has.

—RONALD REAGAN, TO STUDENT GROUP, APRIL 12, 1973

IN BREAKING THE STRIKE OF the air traffic controllers' union, President Reagan in his first year in office sent a clear signal to all federal employees that strikes against the government would not be tolerated. His firm resolve in the face of crisis was noted in many foreign capitals, especially in Moscow.

The nation's air traffic controllers are employed by the Federal Aviation Administration (FAA), a unit of the Department of Transportation. They operate airport control towers and radar centers across the country, and control flight operations to ensure the safety of air travel. Their jobs are essential to the traveling public. These jobs require extensive special training and involve great stress.

In 1981 the controllers, represented by the Professional Air Traffic Controllers Organization (PATCO), made what Reagan and his secretary of transportation, Drew Lewis, considered absurdly high wage and benefit demands. Rejecting a government proposal that would have given the controllers wage increases twice those of other federal employees, PATCO called a strike for August 3. That morning Reagan, flanked by Lewis and Attorney General William French Smith, faced down the union in a short, blunt Rose Garden statement:

Let me make one thing plain. I respect the right of workers in the private sector to strike. Indeed, as president of my own union, I led the first strike ever called by that union. I guess I'm maybe the first one to ever hold this office who is a lifetime member of an AFL-CIO union. But we cannot compare labor-management relations in the private sector with government. Government cannot close down the assembly line. It has to provide—without interruption—the protective services which are government's reason for being.

It was in recognition of this that the Congress passed a law forbidding strikes by government employees against the public safety. Let me read the solemn oath taken by each of these employees, a sworn affidavit, when they accepted their jobs: "I am not participating in any strike against the Government of the United States or any agency thereof, and I will not so participate while an employee of the Government of the United States or any agency thereof."

It is for this reason that I must tell those who fail to report for duty this morning that they are in violation of the law, and if they do not report for work within forty-eight hours, they have forfeited their jobs and will be terminated.

PATCO had either not familiarized itself with Reagan's long-held views about public employee strikes or ignored them. Apparently, they thought he was bluffing. After all, his recent predecessors had frequently given in to public employees' unions when strikes were threatened, and PATCO believed that no president could tolerate the shutting down of the nation's air transportation system. Like many others, before and since, they underestimated Ronald Reagan. He stood fast, agreeing with Calvin Coolidge that, "There is no right to strike against the public safety of anybody, anywhere, at any time." Reagan added, "I also believe that people should keep their word when they make a promise. This is why I fired the air controllers." By the time PATCO realized its mistake, it was too late to save itself or the jobs of its members who had participated in the illegal strike.

Using nonunion supervisory personnel and those PATCO members who voluntarily returned to work, the FAA kept the airlines flying, although at first on a greatly reduced schedule. Flights were kept to a level at which safety could be assured, gradually increasing over the next two years as new controllers were trained and added to the system—a system that, as it turned out, proved safer and more efficient than the one before the strike.

TOP   Reagan discusses the PATCO strike with key aides and officials in the Oval Office

LEFT   President Reagan announces that striking air traffic controllers will be fired

BELOW   With Secretary of Transportation Drew Lewis at the podium, Attorney General William French Smith (left)

REAGAN AND CONGRESS

. . . government is the people's business and every man, woman and child becomes a shareholder with the first penny of tax paid.

—RONALD REAGAN, ADDRESS TO THE NEW YORK
CITY PARTNERSHIP ASSOCIATION, JANUARY 14, 1982

RONALD REAGAN BUILT HIS political reputation as an outsider, a "citizen politician" opposed to big government. Becoming president did not change him. In his first Inaugural address, he pinpointed the source of the nation's troubles in unambiguous terms: "In this present crisis, government is not the solution to our problems; government is the problem."

His favorite government target had always been Congress, which he assailed for its extravagant "tax-and-spend" actions, its unwillingness to tackle the growing national debt, its usurpation of state and local powers, its over-regulation of private enterprise, and its penchant for wasteful, pork-barrel spending to benefit individual members. Congress— controlled for decades largely by liberal Democrats—was vulnerable to Reagan's conservative attacks. When he became president, many in Congress were also collectively angry, unrepentant, and ready to bury him.

Reagan's 1980 victory over Jimmy Carter brought with it a Republican majority in the Senate for the first time since 1955 (although the Democrats maintained solid control of the House of Representatives). But even with a seven-vote majority, the new Senate was not automatically Reagan's. There were no prizes to be won on Capitol Hill by him without a great deal of persuasion and application of all the political pressure his public popularity could muster.

Reagan's toughest congressional opponent was a man with whom he developed a genuine friendship: Thomas J. "Tip" O'Neill, the Speaker of the House. An old-style Boston politician, O'Neill

tried to intimidate Reagan in an early visit to the Oval Office. "You're in the big leagues now," O'Neill told him. Reagan replied that he thought he'd been in the big leagues for quite awhile. He later pondered O'Neill's apparent hostility: "As far as he was concerned, I was the enemy. I guess from his point of view, he was right." Still, Reagan thought they could be friends, but it was O'Neill who set the ground rules. When Reagan telephoned to complain about some unfriendly remarks O'Neill had made about him, O'Neill replied, "Ol' buddy, that's politics. After six o'clock we can be friends; but before six, it's politics."

"Politics" turned out to be six years of unrelenting opposition to Reagan and his policies. But when O'Neill announced his retirement in 1986, Reagan spoke at a dinner honoring him. He said, "[Y]ou know, Tip and I have been kidding each other for some time now . . . A little kidding is, after all, a sign of affection; the sort of things that friends do to each other." Then he said of O'Neill, "You are . . . a leader of the nation, and for that we honor you. But you also embody . . . the hope that is America. So, you make us proud as well, my friend, you make us proud." Jim Wright of Texas took O'Neill's place as Speaker of the House. He was even more political, but not friendly, even after six o'clock.

House Republicans, led by Bob Michel of Illinois, provided only sporadic support for Reagan. In 1981, they collaborated with the Southern Democrat "boll weevils" to pass the Reagan economic recovery plan, but by early 1982 they were attempting to undo the tax cuts they had supported only a few months earlier.

Reagan's diary entry for January 11, 1982, reflects his sense of discouragement: "Republican House leaders came down to the W.H. Except for Jack Kemp they are h--l bent on new taxes and cutting the defense budget. Looks like a heavy year ahead."

The Senate, controlled by the Republicans through 1986, provided more support, even though only a handful of senators identified themselves as conservatives. Among these were Paul Laxalt of Nevada, a close friend since the days when he and Reagan were neighboring state governors; Strom Thurmond of South Carolina; Alan Simpson of Wyoming; Bill Armstrong of Colorado; and Orrin Hatch of Utah.

From 1981 through 1984, the Senate majority leader was Howard Baker of Tennessee, and for the following two years Bob Dole of Kansas (who continued on as minority leader in 1987–88). Neither shared fully Reagan's conservative philosophy, but both worked diligently to give him the congressional support he needed. Baker, for instance, was able to deliver an 89–11 affirmative vote on Reagan's 1981 tax-cut proposal and, later, more than a two-thirds majority in the Senate for a controversial proposed constitutional amendment to require a balanced federal budget. Baker's calm, friendly persistence, combined with unfailing courtesy and a droll sense of humor, made him the ideal person to steer the Senate, just as they later made him the ideal chief of staff to rescue a White House weakened by the Iran-Contra issue.

One of the few Senate Democrats who supported Reagan with any consistency

Conferring with Senators Paul Laxalt and Howard Baker (majority leader), February 11, 1982

The State of the Union address, January 6, 1982

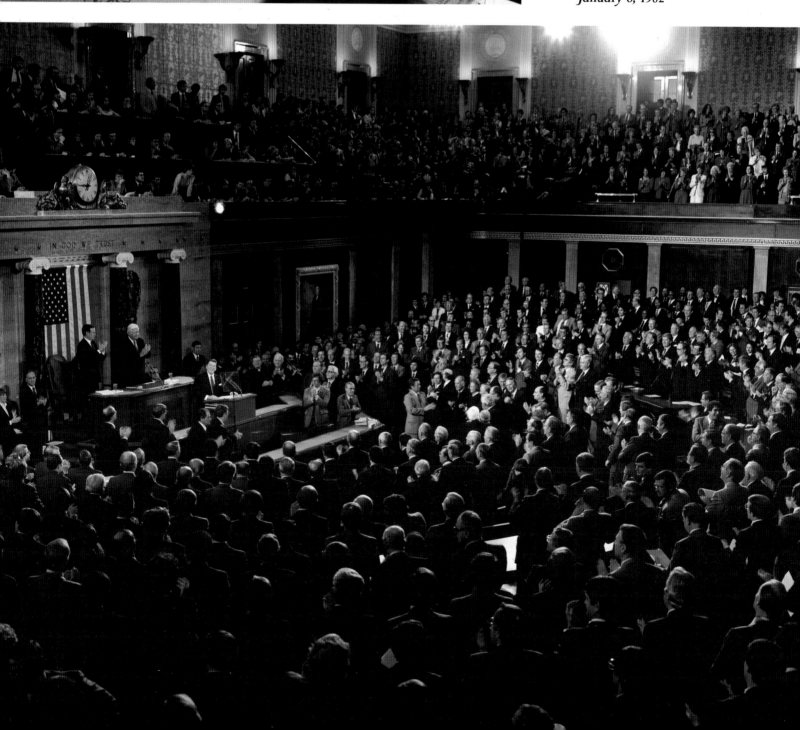

Signing the Social Security bill, April 20, 1983

was Russell Long of Louisiana, son of Huey Long and a powerful and iconoclastic senator. After supporting Reagan's 1981 tax cuts, however, Long, like many others in Congress, got cold feet. Reagan noted in his diary on March 30, 1982: "Senators Bob Dole and [Russell] Long came up to the house to talk the deficit. I love Senator Long and he's a Dem. who has been with us all the way, but now he thinks [the] only answer to the deficit is a big tax raise. I just can't go along."

Another Senate Democrat and a prominent liberal on social policy, Pat Moynihan of New York, was a supporter on some important social issues. In 1983, he was instrumental in fashioning a compromise Social Security reform bill that was a joint product of Congress and the Reagan administration. In 1988, Moynihan authored and effectively pushed through Congress the Family Support Act, which incorporated several of Reagan's welfare reform policies.

The loss of the Senate in 1986 meant

At the cabinet table, with Senator Bob Dole (October 22, 1985)

With congressional leaders (left to right): House Minority Leader Bob Michel, House Majority Leader Jim Wright, Reagan, Senators Bob Dole, Robert Byrd, Alan Simpson, November 12, 1985

that Congress stood, for the most part, united against Reagan during his last two years in office. Under the partisan leadership of Robert Byrd of Virginia and Lloyd Bentsen of Texas in the Senate and Jim Wright of Texas and Dan Rostenkowski of Illinois in the House, Congress engaged in a classic political game: refusing to enact Reagan's proposed spending cuts, then blaming him for the growing deficit.

At the conclusion of his presidency, in January 1989, it could be said that Reagan had more than held his own with an often intransigent, usually difficult Congress. With the help of some stalwart Republican members of both houses and the occasional alliance of some important Democrats, he had passed his eight-years in the "big leagues" with honor and achievement.

A Sunday conference in the residential quarters in the White House with Senators Dole and Byrd and Representative Wright (October 18, 1987)

THE UNITED KINGDOM: "OUR CLOSEST ALLY"

Speaking for all Americans, I want to say how very much at home we feel in your house.

—RONALD REAGAN, ADDRESS TO MEMBERS OF THE BRITISH PARLIAMENT, PALACE OF WESTMINSTER, JUNE 8, 1982

THE STRENGTH OF THE alliance between the United States and the UK during the Reagan presidency was the product of two relationships: historical and philosophical ties between the two nations, and the personal friendship and respect between Reagan and British Prime Minister Margaret Thatcher.

They first met in Mrs. Thatcher's parliamentary office in London in 1975, shortly after she had become the first woman in history to lead the British Conservative party. What was to have been a short courtesy call stretched to two hours, as they matched views on the virtues of free enterprise and ways to reduce government size and influence.

Greatly impressed, Reagan openly expressed the hope that Thatcher would become prime minister. In 1979, she did, leading the Conservatives to a stunning election victory that reversed three decades of creeping socialism. When Reagan became president, his first White House state dinner was held to honor her.

Another early visitor from England, in May 1981, was Charles, Prince of Wales. Nancy had attended his wedding to Lady Diana Spencer the month before, while Reagan was recovering from the Hinckley assassination attempt. Now, meeting in the Oval Office, Reagan found Prince Charles to be a charming and intelligent emissary of the United Kingdom.

The first test of Anglo-American solidarity during the Reagan presidency was the Falkland Islands war. In the spring of 1982, Argentina, then controlled by a military junta under General Leopoldo Galtieri, invaded the Falklands, a cluster of islands in the South Atlantic Ocean, 250 miles off Argentina's coast. Galtieri claimed that the Falklands (called the Malvinas by the Argentines) were historically and culturally part of Argentina, despite their century and a half of British crown colony status. As events unfolded, it became clear that the invasion was Galtieri's last-ditch attempt to save his increasingly unpopular government from collapse.

Margaret Thatcher's response was immediate: She dispatched the British fleet, complete with troop transport ships, to the Falklands, letting Reagan (and, through him, Galtieri) know that Britain

RIGHT A toast to the queen (London, June 1982)

BELOW Welcoming the Prince of Wales to the White House (May 1981)

Addressing the British Parliament in Westminster Palace, June 8, 1982

would use all necessary force to retake and keep its colony. With the fleet underway on its long voyage to the South Atlantic, Reagan and his secretary of state, Alexander Haig, attempted to mediate between the parties. Maintaining an official position of neutrality, Reagan nevertheless let both Thatcher and Galtieri know informally that Britain had his support.

Haig attempted shuttle diplomacy between London, Buenos Aires, and Washington, but to no avail. As the British fleet neared the Falklands, fighting erupted. When Galtieri rejected any settlement short of Argentine sovereignty over the islands, Reagan publicly announced U.S. support for the British. After strenuous fighting, British forces retook the Falklands. Galtieri was removed from power in Argentina and a year later that country chose a new president in a democratic election.

As the Falklands war drew to a close,

the Reagans left for Europe and the Versailles economic summit conference. The first stop was London, where Reagan addressed the British Parliament at Westminster Palace. In that speech, before the ruling body of our "closest ally," he described what came to be known as the Reagan Doctrine: a policy of support for those—anywhere in the world—who fought for freedom and against communism. He said, "Freedom is not the sole prerogative of a lucky few, but the inalienable and universal right of all human beings . . . I believe the renewed strength of the democratic movement, complemented by a global campaign for freedom, will strengthen the prospects for arms control and a world of peace."

Reagan considered this speech one of his most important. It established the principles that guided his approach to East-West relations over the course of the next seven years, and it neatly drew the UK into his worldwide campaign for freedom. The spirit of cooperation and determination he engendered could be seen in his and Queen Elizabeth II's faces as they lifted their glasses in a toast at a

formal dinner following the speech.

In 1983, Thatcher was the host of the economic summit conference in London. There, she and Reagan led the ideological debate for free enterprise and free trade against the socialist president of France, François Mitterand, and Canadian Prime Minister Pierre Trudeau. Three years later, with the American economy booming and Reagan reelected by a landslide, Mitterand suffered the ignominy of having to privatize eighty state-owned companies in the face of a severe economic downturn and the rejection of his party at the polls. At that time, the French president paid Reagan and the U.S. a grudging but great compliment: "Although no system will ever be able to satisfy those who harbor such a desire, I think the American democracy guarantees that the greatest number will enjoy a liberty that is genuine, lived, practical. That isn't bad, even if it remains imperfect. . . ."

On the final night of the London economic conference, the summiteers dined with Queen Elizabeth, Prince Philip, and the Queen Mother. Egged on by Trudeau, Reagan recited from memory the Robert Service ballad, "The Shooting of Dan McGrew," which, it turned out, was one of the Queen Mother's favorite poems. As she chorused "the lady named Lou" with Reagan, the United States and the United Kingdom had never seemed closer.

Reagan and Thatcher were determined to keep it that way. To the chagrin of Reagan aides, such as Don Regan, who felt they should attend the president's every meeting, when Reagan and Thatcher met, they met alone. By their own accounts their conversations were intense, animated, fruitful, and nearly always agreeable. But their minds were not always in tune. In October 1983, at the request of the Organization of Eastern Caribbean States, Reagan ordered a military rescue mission to seize the island of Grenada from Marxist revolutionaries planning a reign of terror against Grenada's noncommunist neighbors.

Thatcher heard about the impending mission, not from Reagan, but from British officials on Grenada, a member state of the British Commonwealth. She was angry and called Reagan to demand that the mission be called off. It was too late: U.S. troops had landed, leaving the prime minister irate and the president somewhat embarrassed—but unrepentant.

With a NASA space station model (July 1984)

With Prime Minister Margaret Thatcher, Camp David (November 1986)

Although troubled by Thatcher's anger, Reagan was certain his decision was correct and that quick action had saved Grenada and the freedom of eight hundred American college students there.

But, for the most part Reagan and Thatcher saw eye-to-eye on the issues of the day. Beyond these, they shared a long-range vision of a world of "peace and freedom for peoples everywhere" and a frustration with those who were reluctant to embrace such a vision. At the London economic summit, when Pierre Trudeau showed his disinclination, Reagan snapped, "Dammit, Pierre, how can you object to that?"

As the years passed and their joint policies proved successful, Reagan and Thatcher's friendship and mutual support grew. When Reagan had surgery for colon cancer in July 1985, Thatcher personally phoned Chief of Staff Don Regan to voice her concern and assure herself that Reagan

was all right. In April 1986, when Reagan decided to authorize a U.S. air strike on Libya, Thatcher supported the use of American bases in England as launch points for the U.S. F-111 bombers. Mitterand, on the other hand, would not even allow the U.S. planes to fly over France.

At their eighth and final economic summit together, Thatcher summed up her own and her nation's feelings about Reagan's America:

Thank you, Mr. President.
Thank you for the summit.
Thank you for your presidency.
Thank you for your testament of belief.
And God bless America.

OPPOSITE **The president and Mrs. Thatcher confer outside the Oval Office (July 1987)**

THE FIRST LADY

Life in the White House is magnified: The highs were higher than I expected, and the lows were much lower. While I loved being First Lady, my eight years with that title were the most difficult years of my life.

—NANCY REAGAN,

MY TURN: THE MEMOIRS OF NANCY REAGAN

UNELECTED, UNAPPOINTED, unpaid, the president's wife nevertheless is expected to be, like her husband, larger than life, always at the top of her form, and flawless in performing her duties—duties nonetheless real for being unspecified. She must exhibit both substance and style and blend them to meet a great variety of difficult and often unanticipated situations.

As wife of the nation's elected leader, the first lady is expected to be a silent partner to her husband and, at the same time, a person of independent thought and action. Reconciling these conflicting traditions—in the harsh, constant light of public opinion—requires that the first lady have confidence in herself and her marriage and know exactly what she's doing.

Nancy Davis Reagan met the test. She was a strong, influential, and effective first lady, but afterward she wrote: "I often cried during those eight years. There were times when I just didn't know what to do, or how I would survive." But, if tough, the experience was also fascinating and rewarding: "I wouldn't trade those experiences for anything. I did things I never dreamed I could do, went places I

At Rancho del Cielo, Santa Barbara County, California

years, had taken Nancy Reagan to task for giving up an acting career to be full-time wife and mother. Now, they objected to the way she looked "adoringly" at the president when he spoke, the "extravagance" of her White House redecoration, the new china, and the borrowed clothes—especially the clothes.

But in the spring of 1982, with one remarkable and engagingly self-deprecating act, Nancy turned the tables on her critics. At the Gridiron Dinner, an annual social event put on by a select club of journalists, and attended by the president, cabinet members, and leaders of Congress, the first lady excused herself from the dinner table, shortly to appear on stage in a fantastic collection of second-hand clothes, in which she sang and danced the old Fanny Brice tune, *Second-Hand Rose*, but with new words:

> I'm wearing second-hand clothes,
> Second-hand clothes.
> They're quite the style,
> In the spring fashion shows,
> Even my new trench coat with fur collar,
> Ronnie bought for ten cents on the dollar.

> Second-hand gowns,
> and old hand-me-downs,
> The china is the only thing that's new.
> Even though they tell me that I'm no longer Queen,
> Did Ronnie have to buy me that new sewing machine?

> Second-hand clothes, second-hand clothes,
> I sure hope Ed Meese sews.

She stopped the show and defused the criticism. In doing so, she also came to terms with the need to pay as much attention to her own public persona as she did to that of her husband.

With the White House itself spruced up and the news media at least temporarily at bay, Nancy turned her attention in early 1982 to a campaign against drug abuse, her "Just Say No" campaign. While federal agencies stepped up their efforts to curb drug smuggling from Asia and South America, the First Lady went after the "demand side" of the

---

never imagined I'd go, grew in ways I never thought possible."

When the Reagans arrived in Washington, Nancy thought her background as the wife of the governor of the nation's most populous state and her nearly thirty-year marriage to a popular public figure had prepared her for the public scrutiny focused on a first lady. But she found out, the hard way, "that nothing—nothing—prepares you for being First Lady. . . . From the moment I walked into the White House it was as if I had no privacy at all. Everything I did or said, whether as First Lady, wife, or mother, was instantly open to criticism—to interpretation, speculation, second-guessing."

The first task she undertook was to put the White House in order—"to reclaim some of the stature and beauty of the building." Many of the rooms needed painting and were sparsely decorated with worn furnishings. The last full set of White House china had been purchased thirty years before, and not enough was left for a state dinner.

Working entirely with donated funds and materials, and scouring the White House storage warehouse in Alexandria, Virginia, for additional furnishings, she had "no desire to turn the White House into an imperial palace," but, instead, wanted to make sure it would "represent the country at its best" to foreign dignitaries and to the thousands of Americans who visited it each day. Her effort was rewarded when Reagan's political adversary, Speaker of the House Tip O'Neill, commented, "You know, I have been in and out of this place for twenty-seven years and I have never seen it look as beautiful as this."

The press was not so complimentary. One columnist carped, "Nancy has used . . . her position to improve the quality of life [only] for those in the White House," ignoring the fact that all the improvements, including a full set of new White House china, had been made at no cost to the government. She was also criticized for borrowing clothes for special occasions from famous designers. Although this is common practice for celebrities throughout the world, her critics judged her harshly.

Throughout 1981 the criticism grew, especially from ardent feminists who, for

---

OPPOSITE As "Second-Hand Rose," Gridiron Club dinner, 1982

problem with a nationwide campaign to convince children not to become drug users. Her campaign was coordinated with the broader efforts of the federal agencies through a White House Drug Abuse Policy Office run by a special assistant to the president.

She traveled the nation, meeting with groups of younger children and organizing "Just Say No" clubs to provide peer pressure and community support for drug-free behavior. Although "Just Say No" was derided as naive by some observers, most hailed it as a simple and effective appeal to every child's need for self-assertion. And, in time, it proved effective. In early 1988, Secretary of Health and Human Services Otis Bowen was able to report the first decline—and a significant one—in cocaine use among high school seniors.

In following years the decline continued, showing that the "Just Say No" campaign had had an impact on the younger children targeted by her campaign. To keep the effort going, she organized the Nancy Reagan Drug Abuse Foundation, which she continued to head after returning to private life.

She also promoted the Foster Grandparent Program, which first engaged her interest when her husband was governor of California. The program recruited senior citizens to serve as surrogate grandparents to mentally disturbed and retarded, institutionalized children. Nancy's interest was in the program's dual benefits: "When you bring these two groups together, each one provides what the other one needs, and everyone is better off."

The first lady was also an important and valued advisor to the president. "Did I ever give Ronnie advice? You bet I did. I'm the one who knows him best, and I was the only person in the White House who had absolutely no agenda of her own—except helping him. . . . I gave Ronnie my best advice . . . whenever he asked for it, and sometimes when he didn't. But that doesn't mean he always took it. Ronald Reagan has a mind of his own."

Most of the advice concerned cabinet and staff appointments. "As much as I love Ronnie, I'll admit he does have at least one fault: He can be naive about the people around him. . . . I don't think Ronnie always saw that some [of his aides] were motivated not by loyalty to their

The Reagans discuss report on drug-use decline with Dr. Otis Bowen, secretary of health and human services, 1988

boss or to his policies, but by their own agendas and personal ambitions."

Perceiving the self-interest of appointees such as Budget Director David Stockman and Chief of Staff Don Regan, Nancy made "no apologies for telling [the president] what I thought," and he clearly valued her thinking. Reagan himself wrote, "I can't say which of us has been right more often than the other. I believe, in general, people are inherently good and [I] expect the best of them. Nancy sees the goodness in people but also has an extra instinct that allows her to see flaws if any are there."

Despite her influence and the public visibility of the programs she undertook, Nancy Reagan remained at heart a private person, devoted to her husband, and relishing most those times when they could escape the public spotlight and relax with one another, friends, and family. Her husband's great love and regard for her was at the center of her life. In his autobiography he confessed, "I miss her if she just steps out of the room." Speaking to a small group of presidential biographers and historians, he said, "You know, if Nancy Davis hadn't come when she did, I would have lost my soul."

Slam dunk!

CAMP DAVID

It was impressed on us from the beginning that Camp David was the president's most private retreat, and that every president who has used it has gone to great lengths to keep it that way. So did we.

—Nancy Reagan, *My Turn: The Memoirs of Nancy Reagan*

For the president of the United States, the light of public scrutiny is nearly always on and the pressure is nearly continuous. For Reagan, "The days I hated most were those with non-stop meetings, one after another, with no time in between to collect my thoughts, and with me scheduled to make remarks or give a short speech at each of them. The days I liked best were those Fridays when I could break away a little early, about three or three-thirty, and take off for Camp David."

During their White House years, the Reagans had two retreats: their own ranch in the mountains north of Santa Barbara, California, and the government facilities at Camp David, Maryland. Trips to the ranch were infrequent, but weekends at Camp David provided a regular and needed respite, if not from work and responsibility, at least from public attention.

A thirty-minute helicopter ride from the White House, Camp David is a cluster of rustic buildings in the Catoctin Mountain Park of northern Maryland. Heavily wooded and remote enough to be secured by inconspicuous perimeter guards, the camp affords the president the luxury of being outdoors without his usual Secret Service entourage. A favorite retreat since the days of Franklin Roosevelt (he called it "Shangri-la"), Camp David is named for Dwight Eisenhower's grandson.

Pat Nixon had told Nancy, "Without Camp David, you'll go stir crazy." Both Reagans agreed she was right. Mixing recreation—horseback-riding, hiking, swimming, watching movies in the

Boarding the helicopter at the White House, bound for Camp David

evening—with work, Reagan found he could get things done at Camp David that he could not seem to get to at the White House. One was responding to letters. From the thousands of letters that arrived each month, volunteers would select two or three dozen each week for Reagan to review, and he answered them during Camp David weekends.

One such letter was from a New York minister who complained of receiving a computer-generated Republican fund-raising letter addressed to "Dear Mr. God." Reagan replied that he had "asked God for a great many things—particularly since getting this job—but never for a campaign contribution. . . . At least the computer has raised its sights considerably; the only other experience of this kind was hearing from a lady whose prize show horse had received such a letter."

There were few visitors other than family at Camp David. On occasion, close advisors were asked to come there for informal work sessions or to brief the president on situations requiring his attention, but not his presence in the White House. Only three heads of state visited Reagan there: President José Lopez

Portillo of Mexico, Prime Minister Yasuhiro Nakasone of Japan, and British Prime Minister Margaret Thatcher (twice).

Each Saturday during his presidency, Reagan delivered a short radio talk to the nation on current issues. Many of these emanated from the lodge at Camp David, where Reagan could sit before the microphones in casual clothes and speak his mind informally to the public.

In the autumn, Reagan would gather Camp David acorns to bring back to the White House for the squirrels outside the Oval Office. And, before leaving the presidency, the Reagans started a fund-raising effort to construct a wooden chapel at Camp David to correct the only deficiency they could find there.

TOP   A Saturday radio talk

RIGHT   Lunch under the trees with advisors (from left) James Baker, George Shultz, William Clark, Edwin Meese

BELOW   Riding with the family

THE GREAT COMMUNICATOR

Some of my critics over the years have said I became president because I was an actor who knew how to give a good speech. I suppose that's not too far wrong. Because an actor knows two important things—to be honest in what he's doing and to be in touch with the audience. That's not bad advice for a politician either. My actor's instinct simply told me to speak the truth as I saw it and felt it.

—RONALD REAGAN, *AN AMERICAN LIFE*

W HATEVER THE MEDIUM — the speaking platform, a personal letter, a cabinet meeting, a newspaper column or radio commentary, or casual conversation—Ronald Reagan will long be remembered as "The Great Communicator." More than any president since Franklin Roosevelt, and perhaps since Abraham Lincoln, Reagan had the gift of clear, pertinent, and interesting expression and the ability to engage his audience—any audience—in both listening and responding to his ideas.

As president (and before that as governor of California), Reagan had too many demands for speeches, brief remarks, and pronouncements of all kinds to write all of them himself. Still, when

Working on the State of the Union speech, January 26, 1982

his writers would present him with drafts, he edited them extensively, invariably improving upon them. One reason for this was that his early career in radio broadcasting gave him a keen sense of how words fall on the ear. Many speechwriters write for the eye. Reagan wrote for the ear.

The speech that first brought him to national attention in a political context was one he wrote himself, in support of Barry Goldwater's presidential candidacy in 1964. What became known over the years as "The Speech" was a *tour de force* given late in the campaign. It drew in $8 million in contributions to the Goldwater campaign and brought Reagan to the attention of his fellow Republicans as a potential governor of California.

In the speech for Goldwater, Reagan displayed an already well-developed skill for using gentle derision; a skill that would later throw political opponents off balance again and again: "No government ever voluntarily reduces itself in size. Government programs, once launched, never disappear. Actually, a government bureau is the nearest thing to eternal life we'll ever see on this earth."

The overwhelmingly positive response of those who heard "The Speech" was, to Reagan, evidence that his thoughts and beliefs reflected those of his audience. "I don't believe my speeches took me as far as they did merely because of my rhetoric or delivery, but because there were certain basic truths in them that the average American citizen recognized," he later said.

Reagan's critics and political opponents consistently missed or ignored this point and, as a result, consistently underestimated his appeal to the electorate. From California Governor Edmund G. "Pat" Brown, the consummate political "pro" who lost his job to Reagan in 1966, to Walter Mondale, whose liberal platform won him only one state in his bid to unseat Reagan in 1984, Reagan's opponents misjudged both the force of his ideas and his aptitude for communicating them.

One reason Reagan has long communicated so well (a reason also discounted by his critics, who tried to portray him as "lazy" or "disengaged") is that he has always worked at it. Throughout his public life, Reagan was an avid reader of biography and history, with an excellent (some aides said photographic) memory. As a political campaigner, he devised an effective short-hand system for transcribing his speeches onto 4-by-6-inch file cards. He would sort and assemble sections from this or that stack of topical references to fit the differing situations and types of audiences he would face from the podium.

When, as president, Reagan faced a workload that required him to rely on his staff to draft most announcements and speeches he was expected to give, he devoted a great deal of time to editing and revising the drafts, making cogent summary statements and phrasing elements of the drafts in plainer language.

Nearsighted (and a longtime wearer of contact lenses), Reagan learned to take out one lens when using a TelePrompTer (or, on the stump, his speech cards), so he could read his speech and observe the audience's reaction at the same time. He was always acutely aware of his audience, remembering those early days as a radio sports announcer. Then, he had improved his broadcasting effectiveness by imagining he was talking to a group of friends gathered around a radio at the local barber shop.

Another reason for Reagan's effective communications is that he consciously developed a style suited to his audience and what he wanted to say to them. His instructions to his speech drafters were: "I prefer short sentences; don't use a word with two syllables if a one-syllable word will do; and, if you can, use an example. An example is better than a sermon . . . Use simple language. Remember, there are people out there sitting and listening [and] they've got to be able to absorb what I'm saying."

Among Ronald Reagan's greatest attributes as a communicator is his sense of humor. Like Lincoln, Reagan is a great storyteller, polished in performance and modest enough to be convincingly self-deprecating. (The self-deprecating aspect often had a beneficial political effect. Before and during the 1980 campaign, he defused his age as a campaign issue by referring frequently to mock personal encounters with figures of long ago.)

From his old friends in Hollywood and

through his own reading, Reagan as president constantly replenished his stock of anecdotes, jokes, and stories. His instinct for when and how to use them was unerring. As a matter of course, he defused difficult situations at meetings with diplomats, members of Congress, or his cabinet with humor, often beginning such a meeting with a story intended both to relax those in attendance and make a point. When he met another storyteller, such as House Speaker Tip O'Neill, he couldn't resist the challenge to trade stories, sometimes for hours, and much to the delight of those present.

RIGHT   Working on the State of the Union speech, January 17, 1985, in the residential quarters upstairs at the White House

BELOW   Sign on President Reagan's desk in the Oval Office

THERE IS NO LIMIT TO WHAT A MAN CAN DO OR WHERE HE CAN GO IF HE DOESN'T MIND WHO GETS THE CREDIT

Taping the weekly radio speech at Camp David (July 23, 1988), ABOVE, and at the ranch (September 4, 1982), RIGHT

Speech at Fort McNair, Virginia, October 25, 1988

RANCHO DEL CIELO

There is nothing quite so good for the insides of a man as the outside of a horse.

—Aphorism often quoted by Ronald Reagan

FOR A MAN IN LOVE WITH THE outdoors, being president was often uncomfortably confining. For Ronald Reagan, "outdoors" was typically a short walk to a limousine or helicopter, surrounded by aides and Secret Service agents. Time for thinking had to be stolen from a hectic round of meetings and ceremonies. Time for contemplation was never on the schedule.

Like other modern presidents, Reagan cherished a private place of escape: Rancho del Cielo, "Ranch in the Sky"— 688 acres high in the Santa Ynez mountains above Santa Barbara, California. Purchased while he was governor of California, the ranch blended land for hiking and riding, magnificent scenery,

good weather, and, most importantly, blessed isolation. "From the first day we saw it, Rancho del Cielo cast a spell over us. No place before or since has ever given Nancy and me the joy and serenity it does."

From Los Angeles the ranch was an easy three-hour drive. After leaving the California governorship, Reagan spent a good deal of time there, working on the property, thinking through his next political moves, and enjoying the beauty and solitude of the place. "Rancho del Cielo can make you feel as if you are on a cloud looking down at the world. From the house we look across the meadow at a peak crowned with oak trees and beyond it, mountains that stretch toward the horizon. From some points on the ranch, you can watch boats cruising across Santa Barbara Channel, then turn your head and see the Santa Ynez Valley unfold like a huge wilderness amphitheater before your eyes."

When Reagan became president, trips to the ranch became less frequent and less serene. Nancy remembers they got there only "three or four times a year . . . [you] could forget the world for a few hours, but every day a government car would drive up the mountain road with a big envelope of mail, security documents, and newspapers." Also, "the ranch contained all the communications equipment a president could ever need," and "even when Ronnie went into the woods, he

would be followed by the Secret Service, the doctor, and a military aide with a portable telephone, just in case."

By 1984, the television networks had found a way to make trips to the ranch even less private: they mounted cameras with telescopic lenses on the mountaintop two miles from the ranch house and telecast live shots of the Reagans sitting at their breakfast table. Since the cameras were on public land, nothing could be done to stop the intrusion, but Nancy retaliated by making up a sign saying "Just Say No" and holding it up when the cameras were on her. "As long as we were going to be on TV, I thought I might as well make the most of it."

Despite their shrinking privacy, the Reagans still found the ranch a break from the pressure-ridden life of the White House, where everything always seemed larger than life and laden with history. In contrast, above the door of the small ranch house was a sign that read "On this site, in 1897, nothing happened," and the sign clearly reflected the Reagans' hope that "nothing" would "happen" while they were visiting.

Their hopes were not always realized: They were at the ranch on August 31, 1983, when Soviet jet fighters shot down a Korean airliner en route from New York to Seoul. All aboard died, including a U.S. congressman and sixty other Americans. Reagan immediately flew back to Washington to take charge of the reactions

of the United States and its allies. The Soviet leader, Yuri Andropov, claimed the Korean airliner was really an American spy plane, but given the circumstances surrounding the incident—Soviet pilots flew near the airliner in bright moonlight for two and half hours—his claim could hardly be given credence.

Reagan's response was firm: restrictions on Aeroflot's landing rights in the U.S. and suspension of several bilateral agreements with the Soviet Union. Nevertheless, it did not scuttle arms control negotiations then underway in Geneva. Although he was criticized by some conservatives for not being tough enough on the Russians, to Reagan the downing of the Korean airliner "demonstrated how close the world had come to the precipice and how much we needed nuclear arms control."

As Reagan explored the defense postures of both countries, he found that "there were still some people at the Pentagon who claimed a nuclear war was 'winnable.' I thought they were crazy. Worse, it appeared there were also Soviet generals who thought in terms of winning a nuclear war." This strengthened Reagan's commitment to the Strategic Defense Initiative.

Another unpleasant interruption at the ranch took place in March 1986, when Reagan's national security advisor called to tell him a terrorist's bomb had exploded in a nightclub in West Berlin, killing an American soldier and a Turkish woman,

and injuring two hundred other people, many of them U.S. servicemen. Irrefutable evidence that the bombing was the work of the Qaddafi government of Libya led to the U.S. air attack on Libya described later in this book.

Not all of the interruptions at the ranch were unpleasant. In March 1983, Great Britain's Queen Elizabeth and Prince Philip visited the ranch where the queen, an accomplished equestrian, looked forward to riding with the president. Unfortunately, the weather turned bad: a heavy rainstorm followed by dense fog ruled out a ride altogether. The royal couple returned to the royal yacht *Britannia*, anchored off Santa Barbara, and took Nancy with them on a voyage up the coast to San Francisco. Reagan joined them there for a shipboard celebration of the Reagans' anniversary. Nancy was delighted. "What more could a girl ask? Ronnie got up and said, 'I know I promised Nancy a lot of things 31 years ago, but I never promised her *this*.' "

Most trips to the ranch, however, were not newsworthy, which is just how the Reagans wanted it. The press, banned from the ranch, hung around the Biltmore Hotel in Santa Barbara waiting for briefings. Reagan staff members and the press drew "Biltmore duty" with some reluctance, because the biggest news of the day typically was a report that the president had cleared some brush and chopped some firewood.

Nevertheless, Santa Barbara was a vast

improvement over retreats of most previous presidents. During his last summer in office, Reagan gave a barbeque for the press in Santa Barbara, and drew cheers when he announced that, on leaving office, "I'm going to start working for a constitutional amendment . . . to make every president spend his vacation in Santa Barbara."

THE HOLY ALLIANCE

You have restored Polish independence from outside influence.

—RONALD REAGAN, ADDRESSING THE MEMBERS OF
SOLIDARITY AT THE GDANSK, POLAND, SHIPYARD,
SEPTEMBER 15, 1990, COMMEMORATING THE
TENTH ANNIVERSARY OF SOLIDARITY'S FOUNDING

AUGUST 1980: SHIPYARD workers in Gdansk, Poland, form the Solidarity trade union and lead strikes in defiance of the Communist government. Ronald Reagan calls the event "the first fraying of the Iron Curtain."

At first the Polish government officially recognized Solidarity as a bargaining unit for the workers, but, as the union became stronger, Moscow stepped in. It installed a military regime in Warsaw with instructions to stop the spread of Solidarity's influence.

Throughout 1981 the situation grew more tense, as Solidarity's leader, Lech Walesa, repeatedly challenged the authority of the government and Moscow repeatedly threatened to crack down militarily, as it had in Hungary after the popular uprisings of 1956. In December 1981, the Polish government, on orders from the Kremlin, closed the nation's borders, arrested Solidarity's leaders, and imposed martial law.

President Reagan reacted with a sharp message to Soviet Premier Leonid Brezhnev, accusing the Soviet leaders of orchestrating "political terror, mass arrests, and bloodshed in Poland." He indicated that Brezhnev's actions "could unleash a process which neither you nor we could fully control." Brezhnev's combative reply: Reagan was acting "in gross contradiction to the elementary norms of international law." Reagan imposed economic sanctions against Poland and the Soviet Union as 1981 came to a tense, unpleasant close.

Although our NATO allies refused to join the economic sanctions, Reagan found an even stronger ally in his efforts to help Solidarity: Pope John Paul II, himself a native Pole. The Pope had already warned the Soviet leaders that if they invaded Poland he would fly there and stand with the Polish people.

Reagan and the Pope began to coordinate their efforts by telephone and through aides. When they finally met in person, in June 1982, both were of a mind to join forces to free Poland from communist rule. The next day, Reagan was in London to address the British Parliament. He reflected both his and the Pope's thinking when he said, "Poland is not East or West. Poland is at the center of European civilization. It has contributed mightily to that civilization. It is doing so today by being magnificently unreconciled to oppression."

The weapons chosen by the Pope and

The "Holy Alliance" is formed. President and Pope meet for the first time (at the Vatican, June 7, 1982)

The Reagans with the Pope, June 7, 1982

the president were neither guns nor butter, but the nurturing of a Solidarity propaganda machine. The tangible aid was equipment: fax machines, computers, printing presses, radio transmitters and receivers, video cameras, telephones, and photocopiers—whatever Solidarity needed to spread its message of worker empowerment and freedom. Priests, CIA agents, along with agents of the AFL-CIO and the European labor movement arranged to smuggle the equipment to Solidarity cells throughout Poland. They also provided the technical and political advice to put the equipment to maximum use. The U.S. Embassy in Warsaw became the most important CIA station in the communist world.

Political pressure forced the Polish government to release Walesa from prison in late 1982. Walesa, in turn, followed the Pope's advice to keep Solidarity off the streets and in the less dramatic—but more effective—business of educating the Polish people to the advantages of

The President and the Pope meet again, in Anchorage, Alaska (May 2, 1984)

democracy. By 1985, several hundred underground periodicals were being produced and distributed by Solidarity, reaching every part of the country. Then, as *Time* magazine put it in early 1992 (the first public revelation of "The Holy Alliance"):

> Step by reluctant step, the Soviets and the Communist government of Poland bowed to the moral, economic, and political pressure imposed by the Pope and the President. Jails were emptied, Walesa's trial on charges of

slandering state officials was abandoned, the Polish Communist party turned fratricidal, and the country's economy collapsed in a haze of strikes and demonstrations and sanctions.

By 1987, Solidarity was strong enough (and the Communist government weak enough), for Reagan to lift the sanctions, and for the Pope to travel through Poland, extolling Solidarity. In 1989 Solidarity was legalized and open parliamentary elections were held. The next year, Lech Walesa became president of a democratic Poland.

REAGAN AND THE WHITE HOUSE PRESS CORPS

. . . I personally liked most of the men and women who covered the White House.

—RONALD REAGAN, *AN AMERICAN LIFE*

RONALD REAGAN'S relationship with the White House press corps was like none other in presidential history. Usually cheerful, optimistic, considerate, and courteous, Reagan was hard not to like, even by reporters jaded by years of contact with beguiling politicians. On the other hand, most of those reporting on his presidency disagreed with his political philosophy and were reluctant to credit his success to his beliefs and actions. Adding to their dilemma was the knowledge that the majority of the public not only liked Reagan, but also agreed with his policies and were suspicious of the news media.

Caught between their biases and their need for credibility with the public, the more inventive correspondents set out to create the impression that Reagan was simply lucky—a desirable trait not associated in the public mind with brains or skill. Illustrative of this approach was *Time* magazine's assertion, in an article otherwise complimentary of the joint efforts of Reagan and the Pope to support Poland's Solidarity movement, that, according to an unnamed source, the Washington-Vatican alliance "didn't cause the fall of communism . . . Like all great and lucky leaders, the Pope and President exploited the forces of history to our own ends."

Reagan remained tolerant and philosophical about the way the media treated him. "When you've been in the profession I was in [acting] you get accustomed to criticism in the press—true and untrue, fair and unfair—and learn to take what you read about yourself and others with a big dose of salt," he wrote. He used humor to deflect importunate questioning. For example, when asked why he didn't try to stop correspondent Sam Donaldson from shouting questions at him on the South Lawn, Reagan replied, "We can't. If we did, the starlings would come back."

The public impression of the White House press corps was gained mostly from televised presidential news conferences in the East Room, where the reporters were freshly groomed and on their best behavior. What the public did not see was the jostling, raucous crew that pushed its way into cabinet meetings or Oval Office ceremonies, shouting questions even when they knew the event was only a "photo opportunity," and grumbling noisily as they were herded out of the room by Reagan staff members.

Bad manners and often biased reporting did not fluster Reagan. Twice a year, he hosted parties for the correspondents and their families—at the White House at Christmastime and a summer barbecue in Santa Barbara. Of these events, he said he had "a very gratifying feeling of shared adventure among us."

"Photo opportunity" in the Oval Office (March 30, 1982)

Secretary of State George Shultz (right) blocks out the noise while the cameras roll (Oval Office, November 20, 1987)

News conference in the East Room, July 21, 1988

FRONTIERS OF FREEDOM

. . . no arsenal or no weapon in the arsenals of the world is so formidable as the will and moral courage of free men and women.

—First Inaugural Address, January 20, 1981

Ronald Reagan's political philosophy as well as his presidency were most clearly defined by his advocacy of the freedom of people everywhere to choose their own government. Throughout, he pursued policies intended to promote individual liberty and democratic governance. Opposed by the entire communist world and by the political Left at home and abroad, he nonetheless had widespread and consistent support among the American electorate, and his policies proved successful.

Margaret Thatcher has said of him,

"Ronald Reagan won the Cold War without firing a shot." His policies were grounded in the belief that there was no moral equivalence in the Cold War confrontation between East and West: "At the level of human values, we were right and they were wrong. Freedom was in every way superior to tyranny. This did not mean that we were perfect, that we wanted war, or that we wouldn't negotiate. But it did mean that we should never blur the key distinction between a free society and the regimented system of our adversaries."

Reagan eventually found justification for

his policies not only in the accolades of allies, but also in the writing of Soviet leader Mikhail Gorbachev, whose 1987 book, *Perestroika*, called for restructuring the USSR's economy to promote individual initiative and entrepreneurship. Reagan exulted: "Although he didn't describe it as such, it was a bill of particulars condemning the workings of Communism, and was as damning as anything ever written about Communism in the West. It was an epitaph: Capitalism had triumphed over Communism."

When Reagan took office, the Soviet Union was following a doctrine laid out by Leonid Brezhnev, who claimed for the communists the right to foment and support wars of "national liberation" anywhere in the noncommunist world and—at the same time—to suppress by force any challenges to communist governments. The USSR and its surrogates were spreading the Brezhnev Doctrine throughout Asia, Africa, and Central America.

One hot spot created by this doctrine was Afghanistan, a mountainous Muslim country, halfway around the world from the United States and little known to most Americans. Using a common border to exploit the weakness of Afghanistan's republican government, the Soviets in 1978 fomented a *coup d'état* and the next year sent in troops to solidify control for their puppet government. In time, the Soviet presence grew to more than 100,000 troops who attempted to subdue the Afghan rebels fighting a guerrilla war from mountain strongholds.

While President Jimmy Carter had signaled U.S. opposition to the Soviet

Voice of America broadcast, September 24, 1983

invasion by putting an embargo on American grain shipments to the USSR and cancelling U.S. participation in the 1980 Moscow Olympics, Reagan shifted the policy to one of more tangible support of the rebels through supplies sent in from neighboring Pakistan.

Gradually, the rebels grew stronger and bolder and the Soviet army began to lose ground. Significantly, the Soviet people back home began to complain about this apparently unwinnable war that was taking the lives of their sons and husbands and weakening their economy. Caught between a worsening military situation and opposition at home, Gorbachev in 1988 pulled out all his troops. A year later, Soviet Foreign Minister Eduard

RIGHT   National Security Council meeting about Grenada, October 23, 1983 (Secretary of Defense Weinberger standing)

BELOW   Meeting with Afghan freedom fighter leaders in the Oval Office, February 2, 1983

Shevardnadze admitted publicly that the invasion ten years before had been a mistake.

Another hot spot was Central America, where Soviet surrogates Cuba and Nicaragua were striving to turn the Caribbean into a Communist sea. The Communist Sandinista government in Nicaragua posed a great danger to its neighbors, due to the nation's size and location. By 1980, the Sandinistas were actively infiltrating El Salvador, Honduras, Costa Rica, and Guatemala. In January 1981 they launched a coordinated and nearly successful campaign to take over El Salvador.

Reagan increased the scope and pace of military aid Carter had begun sending El Salvador. His aim was to prevent a communist takeover, on the one hand, and to convince the Salvadoran government, on the other, to purge its military of extremists, the "death squads" whose savage killing of opponents provided fertile ground for the Marxist insurgents.

Gradually, American aid began to have an effect. Elections for a constituent assembly in 1982 gave power to an anti–Communist coalition. A constitution was drafted the next year. In 1984, with the election of President José Napoleon Duarte, El Salvador established its first democratic government. Duarte remained president until 1989 when, hospitalized in the U.S., he died of cancer, leaving his people a fragile but true democracy.

Reagan's most eloquent denunciation of communism came in a March 1983 speech to a group of clergy at a time when many religious leaders were advocating a "freeze" on the development and deployment of nuclear weapons. In what became known as the "evil empire" speech, he said:

> In your discussions of the nuclear freeze proposals, I urge you to beware the temptations of pride— the temptation to blithely declare yourselves above it all and label both sides equally at fault, to ignore the facts of history and the aggressive impulses of an evil empire, to simply call the arms race a giant misunderstanding and thereby remove yourself from the struggle

The "evil empire" speech, March 9, 1983

With Salvadoran President Duarte, May 24, 1984, after his election.

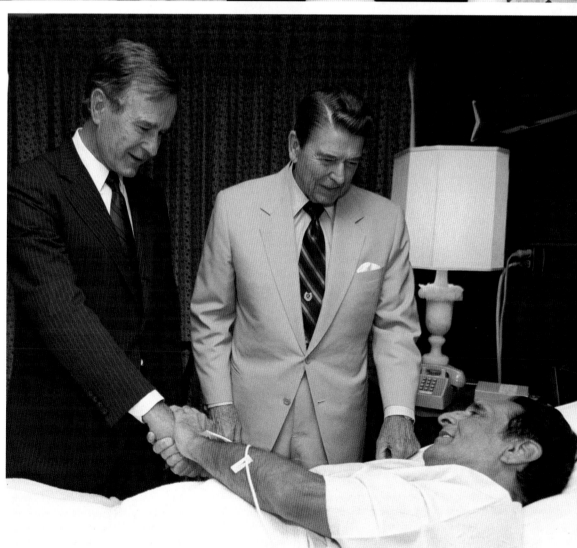

At the hospital bedside of President Duarte (with Vice President Bush), June 5, 1988

between right and wrong and good and evil . . .

I believe we shall rise to the challenge. I believe that communism is another sad, bizarre chapter in history whose last pages even now are being written.

Reagan used all of his communications skills to expose the nature and purposes of the Soviet Union. His policies were carried out by a cabinet team of determined and experienced military, intelligence, and foreign policy patriots, such as Vice President George Bush, Secretary of State George Shultz, Secretary of Defense Caspar Weinberger, and Central Intelligence Agency Director William Casey.

In retrospect, it is clear that by the time of Reagan's first summit meeting with Gorbachev in 1985, the United States and democracy had captured the high ground in the Cold War struggle. And, by the time Gorbachev came to Washington for the third summit in December 1987, the Soviet Union was rapidly sinking under the economic and political pressures largely generated by Reagan. On December 10, during Gorbachev's visit, Reagan marked the anniversary of the Universal Declaration of Human Rights by signing a proclamation in the presence of representatives of ethnic groups from all over the world who had benefited from communism's decline.

Signing the Human Rights proclamation, December 10, 1987

Greeting an Afghan boy in the Oval Office (Rep. David Dreier, center),
January 27, 1988

MASTER OF CEREMONIES

Even after eight years, the experience of walking into a crowded House of Representatives to deliver a [State of the Union] speech sent a chill down my spine.

—RONALD REAGAN, *AN AMERICAN LIFE*

IN COUNTLESS CEREMONIES, often made significant by the simple fact that he is there, the president of the United States defines and reflects the will of the people who have elected him.

Ronald Reagan seemed to be more at home being the nation's "master of ceremonies" than any other president in recent memory. Outgoing and friendly, he enjoyed and seemed to draw strength from contacts with a great variety of people. Whether hosting royalty at a state dinner or meeting a championship basketball team on the South Lawn of the White House, he was interested and interesting, a man who liked and

impressed those he met.

Aware that he, himself, was a symbol, Reagan identified emotionally with other national symbols. "[N]othing thrilled me more than looking up at a wind-blown American flag while listening to a choir sing *The Battle Hymn of the Republic*, my favorite song. On overseas trips I was always moved when I heard our national anthem played at far corners of the world. And I'll never forget standing once in the Vatican after a meeting with Pope John Paul II and hearing a group of American priests singing *America the Beautiful* in as lovely a rendition as I had ever heard. Nancy and I were both in tears."

OPPOSITE, TOP   Honoring pianist Vladimir Horowitz, July 28, 1986

OPPOSITE, BOTTOM   President Reagan welcomes the University of Texas NCAA championship women's basketball team in the Rose Garden (April 16, 1986)

Receiving line, September 10, 1985, with television star Bill Cosby and U.S. diplomat Terence Todman

Cellist Yo Yo Ma plays for then-Crown Prince Akihito of Japan and the Reagans at the White House, October 8, 1987

With the Sons of Lubovitch, December 15, 1987

Proclaiming Adoption Week, Oval Office, November 19, 1987

But it was in the "many, many small moments" of less dramatic events that Reagan found joy in his ceremonial duties: greeting old friends from Hollywood; signing an Adoption Week proclamation, surrounded by adoptive parents and their children; chatting with the leaders of the Sons of Lubovitch, a two-century-old Hasidic Jewish sect from Belorus. He estimated that, as president, he met with an average of eighty people a day, and at some White House receptions he would shake as many as a thousand hands in a single evening. Still, he was able to answer a child's questions that, despite "moments . . . of great grief . . . there were also many moments of great joy, and I enjoyed being president very much."

With the King and Queen of Sweden, state dinner, April 11, 1988

THE FAMILY

Families stand at the center of society.

—RONALD REAGAN, SPEECH, JULY 19, 1982

D ESPITE THE GOLDFISH BOWL aspect of life in the White House, the Reagans never forgot the importance of family ties. All the Reagan offspring— Maureen, Michael, Ron, and Patti—were White House visitors, as were their spouses and the two Reagan grandchildren. The Reagans frequently brought family members together for birthdays, holidays, and other special occasions, as well as for occasional weekends of relaxation at Camp David and Rancho del Cielo.

The Reagans help granddaughter Ashley celebrate her fourth birthday, as her brother Cameron, seven, and parents Colleen and Michael look on (April 1987)

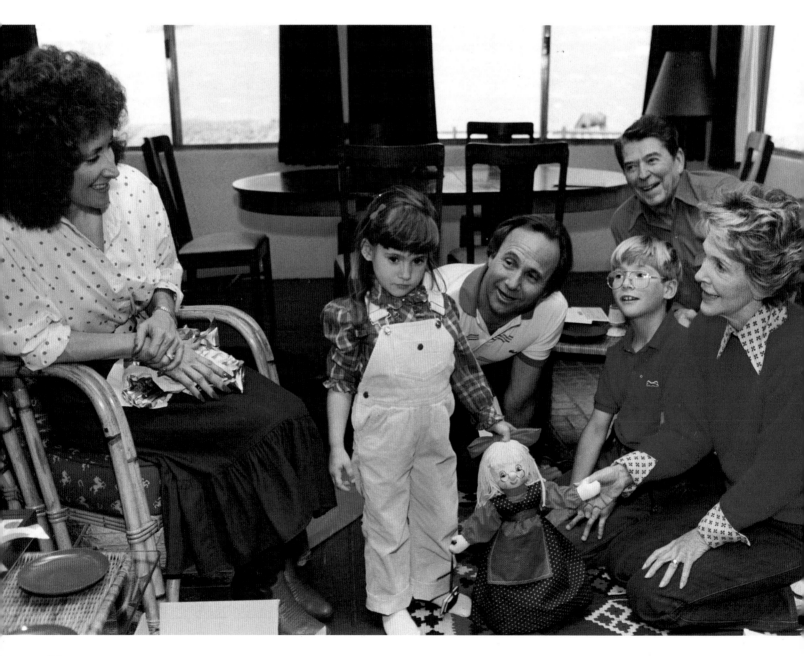

A bicycle built for two: The First Lady with son Ron (April 1981)

Thanksgiving, 1987, at Rancho del Cielo. From left: Dennis Revell and Maureen Reagan, Nancy Reagan, the president, Colleen and Michael Reagan

OPPOSITE Father and daughter: the president with Patti, January 1981

RIGHT Mrs. Reagan visits her mother, Edith Davis, in Arizona in October 1982 (both Mrs. Davis and Mrs. Reagan's father, Dr. Loyal Davis, died during the Reagans' years in the White House)

BELOW Christmas 1983 (from left): Patti, her husband Paul Grilley, Nancy and Ronald Reagan, Doria and Ron Reagan at the White House

TRAGEDY AND TRIUMPH: BEIRUT AND GRENADA

I asked McFarlane how long the Pentagon thought it would need to prepare a rescue mission on Grenada. He said the Joint Chiefs of Staff believed it could be done in forty-eight hours. I said, "Do it."

—RONALD REAGAN, *AN AMERICAN LIFE*

IN ONE SHORT WEEK IN October 1983, Ronald Reagan scored one of his most significant triumphs as president, and suffered his greatest tragedy. The triumph was the military rescue of the tiny Caribbean island nation of Grenada from a revolutionary Communist government; the tragedy was the murder, halfway around the world, of 241 U.S. Marines in a terrorist bomb attack on their barracks in Beirut, Lebanon.

Grenada, independent since 1974, but in 1983 still a member of the British Commonwealth, had recently gone through a bloody political *coup d'état*. The Marxist prime minister, Maurice Bishop, had been assassinated for advocating limited free enterprise. He was replaced by even more radical leftists. Many Cuban workers were on the island, building a large airport and supporting a military buildup with offensive capability. Grenada's neighbors, members of the Organization of Eastern Caribbean States, fearful of an attack, asked the United

States to stop the growing threat with military force. Adding to U.S. concern were the eight hundred Americans attending medical school on Grenada.

When the request came the Reagans were at Augusta, Georgia, for a weekend break. The president was briefed there on a plan for an immediate invasion of Grenada. He later explained, "We couldn't say 'no' to those six small countries . . . We'd have no credibility or standing in the Americas if we did."

Having set in motion the invasion of Grenada, Reagan was jolted a day later with word that a terrorist had driven a dynamite-loaded truck into a U.S. barracks in Beirut, killing 241 Marines. Reagan's satisfaction at having taken decisive military action in Grenada turned to grief at the loss in Beirut of Marines he, himself, had assigned there as peacekeepers. Returning to Washington, he spent the following days immersed in the details of the Grenada invasion. The people of the island nation greeted the Americans as saviors, and the American

medical students returned safety to the United States, many kissing the ground as they got off the airplane.

At the same time, Reagan grappled with the aftermath of the Beirut massacre. He feared—rightly as it turned out—that no response on his part would halt the turmoil that had left Lebanon ungovernable.

All in all, it was a week he could never have anticipated, and would never forget. "[I]f that week produced [through the rescue of Grenada] one of the highest points of my eight years as president, the bombing of the Marine barracks in Beirut had produced the lowest of the low."

OPPOSITE, TOP **With Dominica Prime Minister Eugenia Charles, head of the Organization of Eastern Caribbean States, October 25, 1983**

OPPOSITE, BOTTOM **Meeting with congressional leaders regarding the Grenada rescue mission**

Comforting the parent of a U.S. Marine killed in the Beirut barracks bombing

Memorial service for the slain Marines

SDI—THE STRATEGIC DEFENSE INITIATIVE

Now the world knows that when it comes to our national security, the United States will do whatever it takes to protect the safety and freedom of its people.

—RONALD REAGAN, ADDRESS TO THE
CONGRESSIONAL MEDAL OF HONOR SOCIETY,
NEW YORK, DECEMBER 12, 1983

FOR BETTER OR WORSE, Ronald Reagan's vision for a national defense "shield" against nuclear attack will always be linked to *Star Wars*, the futuristic 1977 space movie. Critics borrowed the title in an attempt to disparage Reagan's Strategic Defense Initiative (SDI), and the news media—always searching for ways to simplify—used it for quick and colorful identification.

Reagan conceived of the SDI early in his first term, but did not announce it publicly until 1983. From then on, it became the most controversial—and perhaps the most influential—defense strategy in U.S. history.

Reagan had long been dissatisfied with the "mutually assured destruction" (MAD) policy that the United States had pursued for most of the Cold War years. MAD perpetuated the arms race with the Soviet Union by constantly increasing the nation's offensive nuclear capability, in order to demonstrate to the Kremlin that an attack on us would destroy both nations. To Reagan, "It was like having two Westerners standing in a saloon, aiming their guns at each other's head—permanently." By 1980, the nuclear forces of the two nations were capable of destroying civilization and perhaps all life on earth.

The president asked his Joint Chiefs of Staff if a defensive weapon system could be developed that could intercept and

Announcing the Strategic Defense Initiative in a television address to the nation, March 23, 1983

destroy nuclear weapons as they emerged from their silos. The answer was that it was worth exploring. Earlier developments of antiballistic-missile defense systems had solved many of the technological problems; however, these developments had been cut off by a 1972 treaty promoted by MAD proponents. In addition to this technology, we had a spy satellite program that provided the basis for embedding a missile-destroying weapon in a working defense system.

The concept was for space satellites to detect the missiles as they left their silos, then trigger their destruction by powerful space-borne lasers. Only the missiles would be destroyed; there would be little or no "collateral" destruction of life or property. We also had in hand the technology for intercepting incoming missiles on the downward stage of their flight. This would provide extra protection in the event a hostile missile had not been destroyed after takeoff or at the apex of its flight by the new laser systems to be developed. The overall system as it was envisioned was simple and effective, but also expensive. Reagan knew the United States was the only nation in the world that could afford to develop it. We had the resources and the know-how. What was needed was the political will to move forward. Reagan supplied it.

He announced the Strategic Defense Initiative program in a television address to the nation in March 1983. He dramatized the need for it with a graphic presentation of the Soviet arms buildup that was giving the MAD edge to the USSR. He also showed how the U.S. defense expenditures (as a percentage of the federal budget) had shrunk in the 1970s, leaving the door open for Soviet military domination.

Reagan then presented his vision of the SDI, not only for the United States, but for all the free world as well. It would be a defense system that "did not rest upon the threat of instant U.S. retaliation to deter a Soviet attack, [but one which] could intercept and destroy strategic ballistic missiles before they reached our own soil or that of our allies."

The SDI became immediately controversial and stayed that way throughout the Reagan presidency—and beyond. Those with a vested interest in continuing the MAD policy (a sizeable part of the scientific community and defense industry) used the media to ridicule Reagan's "Star Wars" program as being technologically impossible and a great waste of money.

The USSR, on the other hand, took it seriously. Mikhail Gorbachev tried his best at the Reykjavik summit meeting in 1986 to bully and cajole Reagan into stopping the SDI's development. Analyzing the costs of developing such a defense, Gorbachev realized that the USSR could no longer compete in the Cold War with the United States without bankrupting the state and risking a popular uprising.

Reagan's rejection of Gorbachev's demands proved a turning point in East-West relations and marked the beginning of the visible decline of communism in the USSR and its European satellites. Realizing that Reagan would not budge on the SDI, Gorbachev knew the game was up.

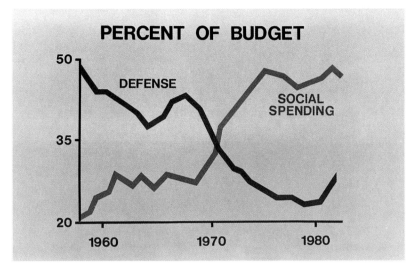

Chart showing nation's defense as a percentage of the federal budget

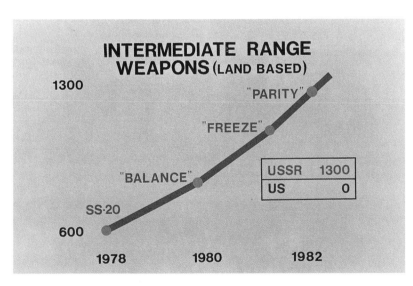

Comparison of U.S. and Soviet missile strength

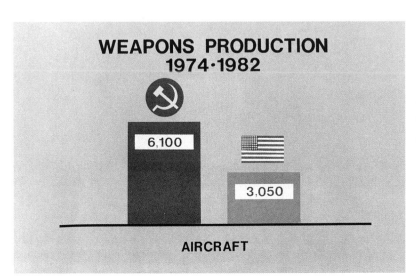

Comparison of U.S. and USSR military aircraft production

A VISIT TO IRELAND

What an incredible country we live in, where the great-grandson of a poor immigrant from Ballyporeen could become President.

—RONALD REAGAN, *AN AMERICAN LIFE*

ON THEIR WAY TO THE London economic summit in June 1984, the Reagans stopped in Ireland to visit the village of his ancestors, Ballyporeen in County Tipperary. Reagan had always been fascinated by—and proud of—his Irish heritage, but without knowing a great deal about it, since his father had been orphaned as a small child. In Ballyporeen he expanded both his knowledge and his pride.

Reagan knew that his great-grandfather, Michael Reagan, had left Ballyporeen for America, one of more than a million-and-a-half Irish emigrants to flee during the potato famine of 1846–1851. In Ballyporeen the local priest led Reagan through the Catholic church that Michael had attended, and showed him the record of his great-grandfather's baptism in 1829.

Reagan then toured the crowded streets of the village, ending up at a pub named for him (at least for the day!). He drank the local beer and was presented with a family tree produced by Burke's Peerage, showing that he was distantly related both to Queen Elizabeth II and John F. Kennedy. He was introduced to several distant relatives, including one young man who could have been a double for the president in his earlier years.

Later he wrote, "So this was home. This was where my people came from in ages past. That's the great thing about being American, we all come from someplace else. We all have roots that reach somewhere far away. Even the Native American Indian apparently came across from Asia when there was a land bridge leading to North American tens of thousands of years ago. We all have another home."

D-DAY—THE FORTIETH ANNIVERSARY

We will always remember. We will always be proud. We will always be prepared, so we may always be free.

—RONALD REAGAN, NORMANDY, FRANCE, JUNE 6, 1984

FOLLOWING THEIR VISIT TO Ballyporeen, Ireland, the Reagans went to the Normandy coast to participate in ceremonies marking the fortieth anniversary of the World War II Allied invasion of Western Europe, "D-Day."

On June 6, 1944, American, British, Canadian, Free French, and Polish troops stormed the beaches and cliffs of this windy coastline to open the decisive phase of the war against Nazi Germany. Superiority in the air, tactical surprise, and a break in the weather combined to make the risky landings successful, but with high casualties.

The Reagans went first to Pointe de Hoc, where 225 American Rangers had scaled a one-hundred-foot cliff in the face of strong German resistance to gain an important foothold and observation point early in the D-Day landings. Casualties exceeded 50 percent. After the war, a thin stone obelisk was erected at the top of the cliff to symbolize the daggers the Rangers had thrust into the cliff as they climbed.

Sixty-two of the surviving Rangers made the pilgrimage to France to mark the fortieth anniversary of their heroic feat. As Reagan stood before the monument and looked over the group of aging veterans, he said: "These are the boys of Pointe de Hoc. These are the men who took the cliffs. These are the champions who helped free a continent. These are the heroes who helped end a war."

With French President François Mitterand at the Omaha Beach Memorial

With D-Day veterans (U.S. Rangers' monument in background)

At the Allied cemetery, Omaha Beach, Normandy

97

TO CHINA

. . . the future is hard to predict in China, although I'm
still betting on the triumph there of the tidal wave of
freedom that is sweeping our world.

—RONALD REAGAN, *AN AMERICAN LIFE*

EARLY IN HIS FIRST TERM, Reagan was pressed by Secretary of State Alexander Haig and Asia specialists at the State Department to improve relations with the Communist government on the mainland of China. Reagan had long supported the Republic of China on Taiwan as a loyal ally of long standing. He was reluctant to back away from the support for Taiwan embodied in the Taiwan Relations Act passed by Congress in 1979.

By early 1984, however, Reagan was intrigued by reports that Beijing was moving toward a free enterprise economy, with foreign investment encouraged. On April 22—Easter Sunday—the Reagans took off from California to see the People's Republic of China for themselves.

Over six days they visited Beijing, Shanghai, Xian, the Great Wall, model villages, and farms and factories. The president gave two speeches, both of which were broadcast (with some deletions). He met with Premier Zhao Ziyang and the country's leader Deng Xiaoping. At the beginning of the meeting with the latter, the diminutive Deng hectored Reagan about Taiwan, Israel, arms control, and other issues. When Reagan returned the verbal fire with corrective data, Deng began to relax and cordiality ruled. He had been testing his guest.

After his return from China, Reagan viewed China with a mixture of hope (that its fledgling economic freedoms would expand) and concern (that its aging authoritarian leaders would not permit political freedom so long as they held power).

On the Great Wall

Addressing a group of Chinese officials in The Great Hall of the People, Beijing

Meeting with Deng Xiaoping in Beijing

FOUR MORE YEARS!

*While we were having dinner, I was called to the
telephone. It was Walter Mondale conceding.*

—RONALD REAGAN, *AN AMERICAN LIFE*

FORTY-NINE STATES (ALL BUT Minnesota and the District of Columbia) reelected Ronald Reagan president by a landslide in November 1984. The Reagan-Bush ticket took 59 per cent of the total vote against former Vice President Walter Mondale and his running mate, Rep. Geraldine Ferraro.

While Reagan held a strong lead in public opinion polls almost from the beginning to the end of the campaign season, he did not take victory for granted. To avoid that politician's nemesis, overconfidence, Reagan set out "to act as if I'm one vote behind" throughout the campaign. He and his staff had cause to worry after the first Reagan-Mondale debate in Louisville, Kentucky, October 4. As candidates and those who work with them know, "overbriefing" is a danger before a debate or other event where spontaneity is important. There is a fine line between having the relevant data ready to be used and "cramming," as if for an exam. The president made some rhetorical stumbles in the debate and concluded that he had been overcoached. The news media called Mondale the victor. Some implied Reagan might be too old to serve another term.

Two weeks later in Kansas City, the rivals met again. This time, Reagan did less cramming. At one point he was asked if he thought age would be a factor in the campaign. Spontaneously, Reagan replied, "I am not going to exploit for political purposes my opponent's youth and inexperience." The crowd roared, Mondale laughed, the television cameras recorded it all, and that was what was remembered about the debate. Reagan regained any points lost in the polls and surged forward to victory.

The Reagans on the campaign trail, October 6, 1984

President Reagan speaks to the Republican National Convention, accepting its nomination for a second term, Dallas, Texas, August 23, 1984

ABOVE   *Reviewing notes for a campaign speech (with aide Ken Khachigian) on the campaign train, October 12, 1984*

LEFT **and** BELOW   *Thumbs up! (Reagan later wrote that one of the things that stood out in his memory from that campaign was the enthusiasm of blue-collar workers that he met "on the stump"), October 12, 1984*

Campaigning in California (Governor George Deukmejian at left), September 3, 1984

Debating the Democratic nominee Walter Mondale (October 7, 1984)

The Reagans watch the Democratic National Convention on television with Vice President George Bush and Barbara Bush, July 1984

LIFE AT THE WHITE HOUSE

I wouldn't complain. After all, when I was a kid we lived above the store.

—RONALD REAGAN'S REPLY TO AN AIDE'S QUESTION,
"HOW WOULD YOU LIKE LIVING THERE?" AS THEY DROVE PAST THE
WHITE HOUSE IN JULY 1978

Christmas season, 1984

THE WHITE HOUSE IS SMALL compared to the palaces of Europe, Asia, and the Middle East. Yet, to most Americans, it is an elegant mansion—a fitting home for the leader of the world's most powerful nation. It is also accessible to the public, as befits the president's home in a representative democracy.

Standing at virtually the center of downtown Washington, D.C., the White House is in plain view of the crowds of people who pass by on Pennsylvania Avenue and the Ellipse. Daily tours of the ground and first floors are open to the public, free of charge. Security is tight, but seldom obtrusive. The Secret Service agents who guard the president, and the National Park Service police who protect the building and grounds are trained to be as courteous as they are diligent.

The Reagans were the thirty-ninth presidential family to occupy the White House. Although George Washington was the driving force in its design and construction, it was completed too late for his presidency. It was first occupied in November 1800 by his successor, John Adams. It has been occupied continuously since then, with two exceptions. It was burned to a hollow shell by the British in 1814 (during James Madison's presidency) and was not fully restored until 1818, when the Monroes moved in. More than a century later, in 1948, deterioration due to age and neglect forced a major four-year restoration and structural modernization. During that time, the Trumans lived across the street in Blair House, the government's official guest house.

The Reagans found the White House structurally sound, but walls, floors, and furnishings were in need of upkeep. Using privately donated funds and furniture stored in federal warehouses, Nancy saw to the redecorating of the White House, beginning with the second floor living quarters, as she put it, to "reclaim some of the stature and dignity of the building. I've always felt that the White House should represent this country at its best."

During the Reagan years there, the White House always was "at its best," but never more so than during the Christmas season when it was "the prettiest house in the land," as Reagan described it. At the annual parties for Congress, the news media, and the White House staff, guests would wander through the first-floor rooms, overwhelmed by the beauty of the decorations. While one or two rooms were specially decorated for other occasions, such as state dinners, at Christmas the whole house was festive.

Reagan gave full credit to Nancy for the beauty of the White House and the efficiency of its operation. But Nancy received her most rewarding compliment from one of the butlers, who had worked there thirty-seven years. She relates, "As he was setting down the tray in front of me, he looked down the center hall, smiled, and said, 'It's beginning to look like the White House again.' I felt as if I had just been awarded the Congressional Medal of Honor."

RIGHT *The Red room*

BELOW *State dinner, April 11, 1988*

Christmas season, 1988

The Green room

The 1988 Christmas tree

The East room, 1985

THE FIRST SUMMIT

We don't mistrust each other because we're armed. We're armed because we mistrust each other. We have two alternatives: to find a way to trust one another enough to begin to reduce arms, or to have an all-out arms race. That's a race you can't win.

RONALD REAGAN TO MIKHAIL GORBACHEV
GENEVA, NOVEMBER 19, 1985

W HEN HE BECAME PRESIDENT, Ronald Reagan inherited the Cold War with the Soviet Union that had bedeviled his predecessors for thirty-five years. Both sides had stockpiled nuclear weapons far beyond the numbers needed to annihilate one another.

The national defense strategy that had produced this frightening prospect was called "Mutual Assured Destruction" (MAD). The concept behind it was that if neither nation could win a nuclear war, neither would start one. Reagan had often expressed dissatisfaction with the MAD concept and with the Strategic Arms Limitation Treaties (SALT), by which both nations sought to limit the growth rate of nuclear arms production. To him reduction of nuclear weapons—not merely limitation of growth—was the proper goal for treaty negotiations, and the proper defense system was one that would actively protect the nation against nuclear attack. His ultimate dream was a world free of nuclear weapons.

From the first, Reagan, as president, initiated major changes in Cold War and national defense policies by strengthening and modernizing the military (particularly in conventional weapons, where Soviet capabilities far surpassed those of the United States and its NATO allies) and by initiating work on the Strategic Defense Initiative (SDI) which would create systems to destroy inbound enemy missiles before they could damage the U.S. He also changed the name of the arms control treaty negotiations from SALT to START (Strategic Arms Reduction Treaty) and said the Soviet Union needed to drop its policy of seeking world domination as a precondition to negotiating a permanent peaceful coexistence. Always, however, Reagan kept the hope that these policies would lead to direct negotiations between himself and the leader of the Soviet Union which would provide the best opportunity for agreement on mutual arms reduction and other positive steps to end the Cold War.

The death of three successive Soviet leaders during Reagan's first term prevented that hope from becoming a reality (Leonid Brezhnev in 1982, Yuri Andropov in 1984, and Konstantin Chernenko in 1985).

Fortunately, the next Kremlin leader,

Reagan, in Geneva, signaling the press as he leaves for his first summit session with Gorbachev

Mikhail Gorbachev, was a younger, healthier man (he was the youngest member of the Politburo). When Vice President George Bush went to Moscow for Chernenko's funeral, he carried with him a letter from Reagan inviting Gorbachev to a summit meeting in Washington, D.C. Gorbachev replied that he had a "positive attitude" toward such a meeting, but not necessarily in Washington. After several exchanges of letters, they agreed to meet in Geneva, Switzerland, in the latter half of November 1985, in what was to be the first of four extraordinary summit meetings between the two.

It is clear from the accounts of those present at Geneva that no one expected substantive decisions to be reached. Secretary of State George Shultz told Reagan that this first summit would be a success if nothing more was accomplished than an agreement to meet again. The agenda was organized almost as a series of formal debates, in which either Reagan or Gorbachev would state a position in support of his nation's policies and the other would make a rebuttal statement.

Reagan, however, had his own ideas on how to break the icy formality of two leaders and their advisors facing each other across a large conference table. During the afternoon of the first day of the summit, a cold and windy November 19, Reagan took advantage of a point in the agenda in which he and Gorbachev would be the only listeners, to invite his counterpart to walk to a boathouse on the Ville Fleur d'Eau grounds for fresh air and a private conversation. There, before a warming fire, Reagan laid out his personal agenda for this and future summits. He told Gorbachev that, as leaders of the

world's two most powerful nations, they were probably the only two persons in the world who could bring about World War III, and possibly the only two who might be able to bring lasting peace to the world. He made the frank statement quoted above, and he concluded that he and Gorbachev owed it to the world to build the trust and confidence in each other that could lead to genuine peace.

Gorbachev responded positively to Reagan, and for the next hour the two men, with only their translators present, explored areas of agreement and differences. By the time they returned to the formal meeting they had committed themselves to at least two future summits, one in Washington and the other in Moscow. And, they had reached an understanding of how they could move toward resolution of their nation's differences.

At the time few recognized it, but in that boat house by Lake Geneva the stage had been set for events that would change the world dramatically.

THE SECOND INAUGURAL

The next day, January 22, it was back to work. On the economic front,
my biggest goal for the second term was to make the federal tax code
less complicated and less onerous on the Americans who were the real producers...

—RONALD REAGAN, *AN AMERICAN LIFE*

F RONALD REAGAN'S FIRST
Inaugural celebration as president took
place on an unseasonably warm day, his
second took place on an unseasonably cold
one. The Constitution required that he
and Vice President George Bush take their
oaths of office on January 20, 1985, a
Sunday. They did so, in the White House,
but the formal outdoor ceremonies and
Inaugural parade were scheduled the next
day. On Sunday afternoon, however,
Inaugural committee officials urged that
the outdoor events be cancelled because
the temperatures would hover around 10
degrees and the wind-chill factor would
be 20 degrees below zero. There would
be serious risk of hypothermia and
frostbite for the young band members and
other participants if they marched. So, on
Monday, Reagan and Bush took their
second oath of office in the Capitol
Rotunda instead. This was followed by the
traditional lunch with congressional
leaders, after which the Reagans went by
helicopter to the big Capitol Center arena
in suburban Maryland where the paraders
from all over the nation were gathered for
a musical gala. That evening, despite the
weather, the Reagans attended each of the
eleven Inaugural balls.

ABOVE *Reagan family Bible used at the*
president's second Inauguration

RIGHT *The Reagan Bible was turned to*
II Chronicles, Chapter 7, Verse 14 (God's
promises to Solomon)

God's promises to Solomon. II. CHRON

LORD: for there he offered burnt offerings,
and the fat of the peace offerings, because
the brasen altar which Sŏl'ŏ-mon had made
was not able to receive the burnt offerings,
and the meat offerings and the fat.

8 ¶ Also at the same time Sŏl'ŏ-mon kept
the feast seven days, and all Ĭs'rā-ĕl with him,
a very great congregation, from the entering
in of Hā'māth unto the river of Ē'ġўpt.

9 And in the eighth day they made a solemn
assembly: for they kept the dedication of
the altar seven days, and the feast seven
days.

10 And on the three and twentieth day
of the seventh month he sent the people away
into their tents, glad and merry in heart for the
goodness that the LORD had shewed unto
Dā'vĭd, and to Sŏl'ŏ-mon, and to Ĭs'rā-ĕl
his people.

11 Thus Sŏl'ŏ-mon finished the house of
the LORD, and the king's house: and all that
came into Sŏl'ŏ-mon's heart to make in the
house of the LORD, and in his own house, he
prosperously effected.

12 ¶ And the LORD appeared to Sŏl'ŏ-mon
by night, and said unto him, I have heard
thy prayer, and have chosen this place to
myself for an house of sacrifice.

13 If I shut up heaven that there be no rain,
or if I command the locusts to devour the
land, or if I send pestilence among my people;

14 If my people, which are called by my
name, shall humble themselves, and pray,
and seek my face, and turn from their wicked
ways; then will I hear from heaven, and will
forgive their sin, and will heal their land.

15 Now mine eyes shall be open, and mine
ears attent unto the prayer *that is made* in
this place.

16 For now have I chosen and sanctified
this house, that my name may be there for

Chief Justice Warren Burger administers the oath of office to President Reagan

The Reagans at an Inaugural ball

BERGEN-BELSEN AND BITBURG

On this fortieth anniversary of World War II, we mark the day when the hate, the evil . . . ended, and we commemorate the rekindling of the democratic spirit in Germany.

—RONALD REAGAN, BITBURG AIR BASE, GERMANY, MAY 5, 1984

IN SPRING 1985, PRESIDENT Reagan accepted an invitation from Chancellor Helmut Kohl to make an official state visit to the Federal German Republic following that May's economic summit meeting in Bonn. One stop on the itinerary was to be a military cemetery at Bitburg, near the Luxembourg border. There, Reagan and Kohl were to take part in a brief ceremony to mark the end of the war in Europe forty years before and the ensuing peaceful relations between former enemies.

After he had accepted the invitation and his staff had confirmed the schedule developed by the German government, Reagan learned that among the two thousand buried at Bitburg were eighteen SS storm troopers, members of the elite group that had staffed the Nazi death camps and carried out the extermination of Jews throughout Europe. The cemetery had been blanketed with snow when Reagan's advance team visited it, so they had been unaware of the storm troopers' graves.

Jewish organizations throughout the U.S. quickly mounted a campaign to persuade Reagan to drop the Bitburg visit. Veterans' organizations, the news media, and most Reagan advisors joined in. Even Nancy opposed it: "I pleaded with Ronnie to cancel the trip. . . . I wasn't alone. . . . Fifty-three senators and almost four hundred members of the House asked Ronnie not to go." Kohl, however, was just as adamant that Reagan stick to his schedule, claiming that a last-minute change would damage him politically and be considered an insult to the German people.

Thus, despite the criticism, Reagan chose to honor his commitment to Kohl, both to spare Kohl embarrassment and,

Speaking at the Bergen-Belsen memorial

more importantly, because "I didn't think it was right to keep on punishing every German for the Holocaust, including generations not yet born in the time of Hitler."

May 5, the day of the controversial visit, was a long one for Reagan and Kohl. First, they stopped at the grave of Konrad Adenauer, who had led West Germany through the years of rebuilding followed the war. Next, they visited Bergen-Belsen, the concentration camp that the Germans had made into a museum and memorial to the death camp victims.

In his comments at Bergen-Belsen, Reagan evoked the spirit of Anne Frank, the Jewish girl who had died there, leaving behind a poignant two-year diary of her family's vain attempts to hide from the Nazis, and an abiding faith that "In spite of everything I still believe that people are good at heart." Reagan's footnote:

"We're all witnesses; we share the glistening hope that rests in every human soul. Hope leads us, if we're prepared to trust it, toward what our President Lincoln called the better angels of our nature. And then, rising above all this cruelty, out of this tragic and nightmarish time, beyond the anguish, the pain, and the suffering for all time, we can and must pledge: Never again."

Then they went on to Bitburg cemetery where they were joined by two surviving World War II generals, Ridgeway of the United States and Steinhoff of Germany, who placed wreaths at the memorial and clasped hands in a gesture of reconciliation. The day ended at Bitburg Air Base, where Reagan met with American servicemen and women and local Germans.

The following day, their last in Germany, the Reagans were thrilled to hear—on a hillside above an ancient castle—a chorus of some ten thousand German teenagers singing *The Star-Spangled Banner* in perfect English. The young Germans had practiced for several weeks to pay Reagan this honor. He wrote later, "After they were finished, I just stood there, listening to the echo of their voices in my mind. If I had opened my mouth I wouldn't have been able to say a word."

Bitburg cemetery (left to right, Reagan, Kohl, Steinhoff)

Memorial wall, Bergen-Belsen

At the Bergen-Belsen museum

MAJOR SURGERY

Please, God, I prayed, take care of this.

—NANCY REAGAN, *MY TURN*

RONALD REAGAN WAS AN amazingly healthy president. With few ailments and quick recuperative powers, he was able to deflect easily— and humorously—his opponents' jibes at his age. He astonished everyone with his rapid recovery from a near-fatal assassination attempt in 1981, and he repeated the performance four years later when he underwent major surgery for colon cancer.

The cancerous tumor was discovered by Reagan's doctors as they were removing a small, benign polyp from his colon (a procedure he underwent without anesthesia). The following morning, July 13, 1985, surgeons removed a tumor and two feet of his large intestine. Before undergoing the surgery, Reagan signed a letter making Vice President George Bush acting president while he, Reagan, was under anesthesia. That same evening, he signed another letter reclaiming presidential powers, thus carrying out— for the first time—the procedure for presidential incapacity in section three of the Constitution's Twenty-fifth Amendment. The surgery was successful, and Reagan's doctors were able to assure him that all of the cancer had been removed. He was pleased at the result, of course, but unhappy at the way it was reported by the news media. He said, " 'The president has cancer,' [the press] wrote. In fact, the president had cancer." When a doctor who had never examined him appeared on television to say, "He probably has about four years to live," Reagan's response was: "Ridiculous!"

His recovery was rapid after a few uncomfortable days. By Wednesday, July 17, he was working from his hospital room with his staff and the vice president.

He noted the first intimations of the Iran-Contra affair in his diary that day: "Some strange soundings are coming from the Iranians. Bud M [Macfarlane, Reagan's national security advisor] will be here tomorrow to talk about it. It could be a breakthrough on getting our seven kidnap victims back. Evidently the Iranian economy is disintegrating fast under the strain of war."

On July 20, six days after the surgery, he returned to the White House. Before he checked out of the hospital, he recorded his weekly radio address to the nation, using his own experience to encourage others to attend to their health.

"It's important to have a checkup if you think something isn't right . . . pick up the phone, call your doctor or your local hospital, and talk to somebody. Just tell them Dr. Reagan sent you."

Several days later, Reagan scheduled a cabinet meeting. The media were invited to photograph him as he walked from the residence to the Cabinet Room in the West Wing. It was the first "photo opportunity" of his return to work. Seating himself at the cabinet table and watching the departing photographers, he grinned mischievously and murmured, "What do you suppose they'd done if I'd stumbled?"

At work in the hospital, following surgery for colon cancer

With Secretary of State George Shultz

With staff members

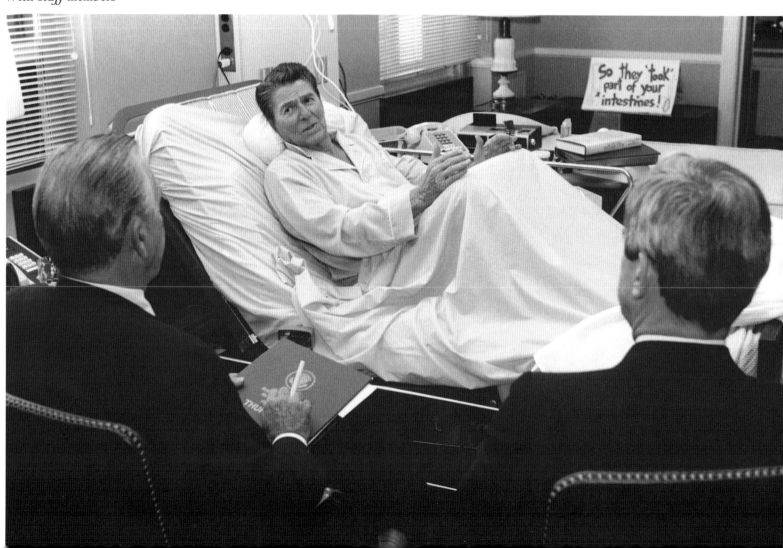

ABOVE   *Arriving back at the White House*

RIGHT   *Recording his radio broadcast from the hospital*

OPPOSITE   *The White House staff welcomes the president*

THE *CHALLENGER* DISASTER

*The future doesn't belong to the fainthearted; it belongs to the brave. The **Challenger** crew was pulling us into the future, and we'll continue to follow them.*

—RONALD REAGAN, ADDRESS TO THE NATION FROM THE OVAL OFFICE, JANUARY 28, 1986

Watching television coverage of the **Challenger** *disaster*

THE YEAR 1986, THE SECOND year of Reagan's second term, was probably the most worrisome of his presidency, encompassing the Reykjavik Summit and the Iran-Contra affair and beginning, on January 28, with the explosion—shortly after takeoff—of the space shuttle *Challenger*. All seven astronauts aboard were killed instantly. Among them was a schoolteacher, Christine McAuliffe, who had been chosen to experience and record for other teachers and their students the work and feelings of the astronauts. Reagan had announced the selection of this first "nonprofessional" astronaut, and this made the tragedy "seem even closer and sadder" to him as he "watched [on television] the film of the explosion played and replayed and replayed again."

The president had been scheduled to deliver the State of the Union address that evening, but he cancelled it and instead spoke briefly to the nation from the Oval Office:

I've always had great faith in and respect for our space program, and what happened today does nothing to diminish it. We don't hide our space program. We don't keep secrets and cover things up. We do it all up front and in public. That's the way freedom is, and we wouldn't change it for a minute.

We'll continue our quest for space. There will be more shuttle flights and more shuttle crews and yes, more volunteers, more civilians, more teachers in space. Nothing ends here; our hopes and our journeys continue.

He ended his address by invoking a poem known to most airmen:

The crew of the . . . *Challenger* honored us by the manner in which they lived their lives. We will never forget them, nor the last time we saw them, this morning, as they prepared for their journey and waved good-by and "slipped the surly bonds of earth" to "touch the face of God."

Three days later, the Reagans attended the memorial service at the Johnson Space Center in Houston. The president quoted a passage from H.G. Wells that Michael Smith, one of the astronauts who died, had written down before the flight.

For man, there is no rest and no ending. He must go on—Conquest beyond Conquest. This little planet and its winds and ways, and all the laws of mind and matter that restrain him. Then the planets about him, and, at last out across the immensity to the stars. And when he has conquered all the depths of space and all the mysteries of time—still he will be but beginning.

The space shuttle program was set back severely by the tragedy, and the next shuttle did not fly until September 1988, three months before Reagan left office. He watched the launching on television, standing with jaw and hands clenched with concern until he could see that it was a success.

*News conference,
January 28, 1986*

*The Reagans comfort
families of the astronauts*

*The first post-
Challenger space
shuttle lifts off,
September 29, 1988*

THE RAID ON LIBYA

. . . an unpredictable fanatic . . . [who] believed any act, no matter how vicious or cold-blooded, was justified to further his goals.

—RONALD REAGAN ON MUAMMAR AL-QADDAFI, IN *AN AMERICAN LIFE*

QADDAFI, LIBYA'S DICTA-tor, was a constant thorn throughout Reagan's presidency. Qaddafi dreamed of uniting the Muslim world as a military theocracy in order to oppose and overthrow governments run by "infidels." His weapons were oil, Soviet military aid, and terrorism.

In May 1981, when the FBI linked a Libyan terrorist to a murder in Chicago, Reagan closed the Libyan Embassy in Washington, D.C. In August that year, during American naval exercises in the Mediterranean, Libyan aircraft fired at carrier-based U.S. jet fighters over international waters. Acting under Reagan's orders, the American jets pursued the Libyan planes and downed two of them.

A few days later, Reagan was told that Qaddafi had vowed to assassinate him and had smuggled terrorist hit squads into the U.S. for the purpose. Egypt's president, Anwar Sadat, whom Reagan considered both a friend and ally, was assassinated in October 1981, and Reagan was convinced that Qaddafi was behind the deed.

By 1986, Qaddafi had become even bolder. Ignoring the internationally recognized twelve-mile offshore limit for sovereignty, Qaddafi established what he called a "line of death" one hundred miles off Libya's shores. He defied anyone to cross it. When the U.S. navy, during its annual maneuvers, did just that, Qaddafi attacked U.S. aircraft with missile-firing boats. The Americans sank the boats and destroyed their missile-guidance radar site. Two weeks later, Qaddafi's terrorists blew up a popular disco in West Berlin, killing one American soldier and injuring fifty others, along with two hundred non-Americans.

Reagan decided he "had to do something about that crackpot in Tripoli." He ordered an air attack on Qaddafi's military headquarters. Land-based aircraft from England and carrier-based ones from the Mediterranean carried out a successful

Speech in hand, the president heads to the Oval Office

Reagan confers with congressional leaders prior to the raid on Tripoli (April 14, 1986)

Addressing the nation from the Oval Office

attack on April 14, 1986. Reagan explained the attack in an address to the nation from the Oval Office:

> We tried quiet diplomacy, public condemnation, economic sanctions and demonstrations of military force. None succeeded. Despite our repeated warnings, Qaddafi continued his reckless policy of intimidation, his relentless pursuit of terror. He counted on America to be passive. He counted wrong.
>
> I warned that there should be no place on earth where terrorists can rest and train and practice their deadly skills. I meant it. I said that we would act with others, if possible, and alone if necessary, to insure that terrorists have no sanctuary anywhere. Tonight, we have.

Although elements of the news media were critical (and media coverage tended to dwell on the few Libyan civilian casualties of the raid), the American public was overwhelmingly supportive of Reagan's action. And, despite gloomy predictions Qaddafi would accelerate his terrorist activities, the reverse was true. Qaddafi never again challenged Reagan, preferring instead to bide his time until the United States might elect a less determined president.

THE STATUE OF LIBERTY CENTENNIAL

I told Nancy, "This is the other woman in my life."

—RONALD REAGAN, *SPEAKING MY MIND*

S HE WAS READY TO BE unveiled by Independence Day 1986— "Lady Liberty," who, for a century had welcomed immigrants by the thousands to America as they entered New York harbor. Originally a gift of the people of France to the people of the United States, the statue had undergone top-to-bottom restoration, thanks to a successful national fund-raising drive. A team of French artisans joined an American team to complete the restoration work.

The centennial was marked by a series of gala events—with flags, bands, tall ships, and thousands of people participating, including President and Madame Mitterand of France. The climactic event took place the evening of July 3. "This was one of the grandest occasions I attended while I was president. What an uplifting experience unveiling the spruced-up lady and relighting her torch," President Reagan recalled later.

In his remarks before turning the switch that lit again "the light beside the golden door," Reagan concluded, "We're bound together because we . . . dare to hope . . . that our children will always find here the land of liberty . . . We dare to hope, too, that we'll understand our work can never be truly done until every man, woman, and child shares in our gift, in our hope, and stands with us in the light of liberty—the light that, tonight, will shortly cast its glow upon her, as it has upon us for two centuries, keeping faith with a dream of long ago and guiding millions still to a future of peace and freedom."

THE REYKJAVIK SUMMIT

At Reykjavik, my hopes for a nuclear-free world soared briefly, then fell during one of the longest, most disappointing—and ultimately angriest—days of my presidency.

—RONALD REAGAN, *AN AMERICAN LIFE*

ON LESS THAN A MONTH'S notice, the Reykjavik Summit was convened at Mikhail Gorbachev's request. It was Reagan's second face-to-face meeting with the Soviet leader. In a long and somewhat importunate letter to Reagan Gorbachev laid out the proposed agenda: weapons in space, medium-range nuclear missiles in Europe, and continued testing of nuclear weapons. Gorbachev insisted on a "neutral" setting for the meeting. Reagan opted for Iceland. The meeting was not to be a formal summit, with all its pomp and ceremony, but rather one devoted entirely to work sessions.

They met on October 11 and 12, 1986, in a private home in Iceland's capital, Reykjavik, overlooking the North Atlantic ocean. The meetings included just the two leaders, Soviet Foreign Minister Eduard Shevardnadze and U.S. Secretary of State George Shultz, and interpreters. From the start, Reagan was encouraged. On the first day, Gorbachev agreed to the rapid elimination of nuclear missiles in Europe and to the eventual elimination—over ten years—of all ballistic missiles. To allay Gorbachev's concerns about the Strategic Defense Initiative, Reagan's space-based ballistic missile defense system, Reagan offered to share SDI technology with the Soviet Union and the rest of the world, and to refrain from deploying the SDI unilaterally for ten years.

On the second day, Gorbachev offered drastic reductions in the USSR's conventional forces: reductions that would guarantee the safety of Western Europe during and after the nuclear missile phase-down. Reagan was astonished and delighted: "As evening approached, I thought to myself: Look what we have accomplished—we have negotiated the most massive weapons reduction in history. I thought we were in complete agreement . . ."

Then, counting on Reagan's euphoria to soften the blow, Gorbachev smiled and said: "This all depends, of course, on you giving up SDI."

Shocked at this about-face, Reagan tried to reason with Gorbachev, reminding him again that the United States would share its SDI technology with him and the rest of the world. He asked, "If you are willing to abolish nuclear weapons, why are you so anxious to get rid of a defense against nuclear weapons?"

Gorbachev, still smiling, countered that he did not believe Reagan's pledge that the U.S. would share SDI technology with the world. For Reagan, that did it. He now realized that Gorbachev had come to Iceland for just one reason: to kill the Strategic Defense Initiative. Reagan stood up and said, "The meeting is over. Let's go, George [Shultz], we're leaving."

Outside, as they parted, an obviously anxious Gorbachev said, "I don't know what else I could have done." A very angry Reagan replied, "I do. You could have said 'yes.' "

In retrospect, the Reykjavik Summit was the final and decisive "battle" in the Cold War—a battle Reagan won for the West. Gorbachev had realized that the USSR could not continue the arms race. It could not afford to develop its own space-based missile defense system, keep up the growth of its conventional and nuclear arms, and still meet the demands of the people of the Soviet Union for material well-being and a better life. At Reykjavik, he played the hand he had been dealt, but it was not a winning hand.

Back in Washington, Reagan briefed the leaders of Congress on the Reykjavik talks, and then addressed the nation from the Oval Office. Despite his anger and disappointment, he understood that Reykjavik had been a turning point, that ". . . unlike [in] the past, we're dealing now from a position of strength. Our ideas are out there on the table. They won't go away."

OPPOSITE:

ABOVE LEFT *The first session in Reykjavik, October 11, 1986*

ABOVE RIGHT *An angry goodbye*

BELOW *Reagan briefs congressional leaders (House Speaker "Tip" O'Neill to his right), October 14, 1986*

THE IRAN-CONTRA AFFAIR

*Now what should happen when you make a mistake is
this: You take your knocks, you learn your lessons, and
then you move on.*

—RONALD REAGAN, TELEVISED ADDRESS
TO THE NATION, MARCH 4, 1987

A MISTAKE IT (OR THEY)
proved to be, but these two
initiatives did not seem so when they
began, and underlying them were positive
motives on the president's part. The first
began as an earnest—though covert—
effort to secure the freedom of American
hostages in the Middle East. The president
was actively involved in approving the
major steps taken. The second initiative,
arming the *contras* in Nicaragua, fulfilled
an oft-stated desire on Reagan's part to
help these fighters for democracy against
the Marxist Sandinistas, but the activities
to achieve this aim were undertaken, he
insisted, without his knowledge.

Throughout the mid-1980s, Reagan and
the House of Representatives, controlled
by the Democrats, battled over funds for
the *contras*. Reagan's frustration mounted
when popular Speaker "Tip" O'Neill
asked his colleagues to vote against *contra*
aid as a retirement gift to him in 1986.
Reagan vowed to do everything possible,
within the law, to keep the *contras* alive
while he fought to reinstate aid.

The threat to democracy in Central
America was clear to Reagan. The Soviet
Union supplied Cuba; Cuba helped the
Sandinistas; the Sandinistas supplied the
Marxist rebels in El Salvador. He was
puzzled that some Democrats in Congress
chose to ignore the evidence. On the
other hand, there was plenty of sentiment

BELOW *In the White House Situation
Room, November 12, 1986*

OPPOSITE:
ABOVE *Meeting with Republican
congressional leaders in the Oval Office,
February 27, 1987 (seated clockwise from
left): Sen. Alan Simpson (R-WY), Rep.
Robert Michel (R-IL), President Reagan,
Sen. Robert Dole (R-KS), Rep. Dick
Cheney (R-WY), W. Dennis Thomas,
assistant to the president, and Frank
Carlucci, assistant to the president for
national security affairs*

BELOW *The president greets released
hostage David Jacobsen, November 7,
1986*

in the United States for support of the *contras*. Reagan wanted those who wanted to help to know where to turn. He also wanted several friendly foreign governments to know the depth of his commitment to strengthening democracy in the hemisphere.

Later there was much debate over whether Congress's Boland amendment—prohibiting the involvement of U.S. government agencies from aiding the *contras*—applied to the National Security Council, a unit of the White House. Reagan's objective—keeping the *contras* alive—was translated by some in the NSC, notably Lt. Colonel Oliver North, into the creation of a network of supplies to the beleaguered prodemocracy fighters. Whether CIA Director William Casey knew of this plan or participated in it will

never be known. He died in May 1987 of a brain tumor.

Back in July 1985, Reagan's national security advisor, Robert "Bud" McFarlane, told him that a group of Iranians had passed on to Israeli sources a message to the effect that they wanted quietly to make contact with U.S. officials in order to discuss ways and means of reestablishing diplomatic relations following the death of the Ayatollah Khomeini. McFarlane asked Reagan's permission to meet with these Iranians. Reagan agreed. What ensued was a series of meetings that led to negotiations for the release of Americans held hostage by Hezbollah, a group presumably subject to influence from Iran. For their part, the Iranians asked the U.S. side to prove its sincerity by allowing Israel to sell them a

small supply of American-built TOW missiles, to be replaced by new ones from the United States. Reagan rejected this idea at first, but was assured that the Israelis vouched for the antiterrorist credentials and moderation of their Iranian contacts. After the first shipment of missiles was made, one hostage was released. The Iranians needed more, they said, to get the other six released.

Reagan's secretaries of state and defense, George Schulz and Casper Weinberger, opposed this transaction, questioning its legality. Reagan, focused on getting the hostages released, considered it acceptable because of the special circumstances. What he did not know was that the revenue for replacement missiles, coming back through Israel, contained a hefty markup and that this profit was

Jacobsen speaks to the news media

Reagan discusses the unfolding Iran-Contra matter with aides, November 25, 1986

Reagan and Attorney General Meese hold a news conference after Meese reports his findings to the president (November 25, 1986)

being used to fund assistance to the *contras*.

The two elements began to fuse together shortly after the Sandinistas shot down a *contra* supply plane on October 5, 1986. Papers on the aircraft implicated the

---

OPPOSITE:

ABOVE   *David Abshire, brought in to coordinate Reagan administration activities in response to the Iran-Contra revelations (January 6, 1987)*

BELOW   *The Tower Commission unveils its report, February 26, 1987 (from left, Reagan, Edmund Muskie, John Tower, Brent Scowcroft)*

CIA. Then, on November 3, a Beirut magazine published a story to the effect that the United States was selling arms in exchange for hostages. The U.S. media jumped on the story.

Later in the month, Attorney General Ed Meese, after conducting a weekend review of all elements of the issue, told the president that a memorandum indicated that Colonel Oliver North, while working on the release of the hostages, had diverted some of the Iranian money to pay for weapons for the *contras*.

Next came the president's Tower Commission, headed by former Sen. John Tower. Then a congressional investigation and nationally televised hearings. Some congressional Democrats could scarcely contain their glee that the Iran-Contra affair might so damage the Republicans that they would lose the White House in

1988. If nothing else, the hearings underscored the on-going struggle by Congress to reduce the powers of the executive branch.

Although McFarlane and his successor, John Poindexter, along with North, were convicted of violations of the law, these convictions were later overturned. Reagan, sharply criticized in the media for failing to exert hands-on management of both matters, accepted responsibility for the mistakes, but made the point that a president must oversee many issues and cannot micromanage all of them.

A special prosecutor, Lawrence Walsh, continued an investigation of the affair over the next five years, spending millions of tax dollars and producing virtually nothing. On balance, what came to be known as the Iran-Contra affair marked the low point of the Reagan years.

National Security Advisor Carlucci and General Colin Powell

ATTACK ON THE USS *STARK*

*. . . there were attempts by Iran and Iraq to close the
Persian [Arabian] Gulf to shipping, while we were
determined to keep the sea lanes open . . .*

—RONALD REAGAN, *AN AMERICAN LIFE*

WAR BETWEEN IRAN AND Iraq raged throughout nearly all of Reagan's presidency, beginning a month before his first election, and ending in a cease-fire only four months before he left office. Throughout this war the United States maintained a studied neutrality toward the two countries, thankful that the equivalence of their forces kept their tyrannical leaders—Iran's Ayatollah Khomeini and Iraq's Saddam Hussein— from attacking other, weaker neighbors.

Iraq financed its war machine with its extensive oil reserves, shipping crude to world markets through the Persian (Arabian) Gulf, its only path to the sea. Iran was not as oil-rich, but it controlled the entire north shore of the Gulf. As the war dragged on, and as Iran realized it could not match indefinitely Iraq's military spending, it threatened to shut down the movement of oil tankers through the Straits of Hormuz, the narrow passage leading to the Gulf of Oman and thence the Indian Ocean. Such a move would have blocked oil shipments not only from Iraq, but also from Kuwait and Saudi Arabia, precipitating a worldwide oil shortage and dramatic price increases in gasoline and other fuel oils.

Reagan saw this threat as one he could not ignore. He pledged the U.S. navy to keep the Straits of Hormuz and the Gulf open to oil tanker traffic. American ships had patrolled the Gulf since 1949 and Reagan saw his move as an extension of previous U.S. commitments to the free flow of oil to the world.

Tension was high in the Gulf, however, and on May 17, 1987, an Iraqi jet fighter fired two missiles into the American missile frigate USS *Stark*, apparently thinking the *Stark* was a blockading Iranian ship. Thirty-seven American sailors were killed.

Five days later the Reagans attended a memorial service for the dead sailors in Jacksonville, Florida. In addressing their families and fellow crew members, Reagan invoked the sentiments of Lincoln's Gettysburg Address, emphasizing the importance of this seemingly minor incident in the greater scheme of things:

Situation Room, the White House,
May 19, 1987: President Reagan asks a
*question about the **Stark** of Gen. Robert*
T. Herres, vice chairman of the Joint
Chiefs of Staff (Secretary of Defense
Caspar Weinberger looks on)

Peace is at stake here, and so, too, is our own nation's security and our freedom. Were a hostile power ever to dominate this strategic region and its resources, it would become a chokepoint for freedom—that of our allies and our own. And that's why we maintain a naval presence there. Our aim is to prevent, not to provoke, wide conflict, to save the many lives that further conflict would cost us.

The fallen sailors of the USS *Stark* understood their obligations; they knew the importance of their job . . . So, it's a simple truth we reaffirm here today: Young Americans . . . gave up their lives so that the terrible moments of the past would not be repeated, so that wider war and greater conflict could be avoided, so that thousands, and perhaps millions, of others might be spared the final sacrifices these men so willingly made.

Coming at a time when the Iran-Contra issue was still daily news, the *Stark* incident served to point up the constant foreign policy dilemma posed by the Middle East to the United States and the other oil-dependent industrial nations of the world.

At the memorial service for the dead American sailors, Jacksonville, Florida

Lunch with armed services members at Camp David, May 23, 1987

AT THE BRANDENBURG GATE, BERLIN

Mr. Gorbachev, open this gate! Mr. Gorbachev, tear down this wall!

—RONALD REAGAN, REMARKS AT THE
BRANDENBURG GATE, JUNE 12, 1987

IN THE SOVIET UNION, THE *glasnost* genie was spreading, people were demanding more freedom, a better life. The threat of an effective American missile defense—the Strategic Defense Initiative—had told Gorbachev his hand was being called. He could not match it without bankrupting his economy. Throughout the Soviet Empire the system that had created the Berlin Wall was cracking, but in Germany the Wall itself still divided a nation, a people, and still symbolized the division of East from West.

Standing before the long-closed Brandenburg Gate and the Berlin Wall, Reagan addressed a crowd that included Chancellor Helmut Kohl and the mayor of Berlin. He spoke of the Wall as a symbol of division between the free world and the totalitarian world of communism and of his hopes of ending that division. "Today represents a moment of hope," he said. "We in the West stand ready to cooperate with the East to promote true openness, to break down barriers that separate people, to create a safer, freer world. And surely there is no better place than Berlin, the meeting place of East and West, to make a start."

In concluding, he quoted a graffiti spray-painted on the Berlin Wall: "This wall will fall. Beliefs become reality. Yes, across Europe, this wall will fall. For it cannot withstand faith; it cannot withstand truth. The wall cannot withstand freedom."

Less than two years later, his prophecy came true; the Wall came down and, with it, communism.

Arriving in Berlin, June 12, 1987

ABOVE *Looking down on the Berlin Wall*

CENTER AND BELOW
Speaking to the German people from in front of the Brandenburg Gate

THE WASHINGTON, D.C., SUMMIT

I think Gorbachev was ready to talk the next time we met—in Washington—because we had walked out on him at Reykjavik and gone ahead with the SDI program.

—RONALD REAGAN, *AN AMERICAN LIFE*

IN DECEMBER 1987—MORE than a year after Reykjavik and a few months after Reagan had challenged Mikhail Gorbachev to tear down the Berlin Wall—the two held their third summit meeting, in Washington D.C.

At the first summit, Gorbachev had accepted Reagan's invitation to come to the United States in 1987, but the stand-off at Reykjavik triggered a series of delays, as Gorbachev continued to insist that the United States give up development of a space-missile defense system (SDI), and as Reagan continued to refuse.

On other fronts, however, there was growing evidence of the Soviet Union's desire (in retrospect, its dire need) to end the Cold War. Russian dissidents were, one by one, allowed to emigrate to the West. Gorbachev announced the first free elections in the USSR since the 1917 communist revolution, and his government began to encourage the establishment of some private business enterprises. Negotiations between the Soviet Union and the United States to eliminate intermediate-range nuclear missiles in Europe (one day to be the INF Treaty) made slow but steady progress.

By mid-October 1987, however, no definite plans for a summit had been made. It was a time when Reagan was beset with other concerns, both presidential and personal. On October 17, Nancy underwent surgery for breast cancer. On October 19, the stock market recorded its largest one-day drop in prices since 1914, sending a great shock wave

through the economy. Reagan's latest nomination for the Supreme Court, Judge Robert Bork, appeared headed for defeat in the U.S. Senate, in the face of acrimonious debate and a highly partisan campaign to discredit the jurist. Then, on October 26, only four days after Nancy had come home from the hospital, the Reagans learned that her mother had died in Phoenix, Arizona.

Just hours before the Reagans were to leave for Phoenix, Secretary of State George Shultz was informed that Soviet Foreign Minister Eduard Shevardnadze was

on his way to the United States to arrange a summit meeting and negotiate the final details of the INF Treaty.

The president cut short his stay in Phoenix, leaving Nancy there to prepare for her mother's funeral. He met with Shevardnadze on October 30, and received a "statesmanlike" letter from Gorbachev, proposing a December summit at which the two leaders would sign the INF Treaty, announce the beginning of talks aimed at a 50 percent reduction in intercontinental ballistic missiles (ICBMs), and agree to a spring

U.S. and Soviet flags bedeck the Old Executive Office Building for the Washington summit, December 8, 1987

U.S. arms negotiators meet with President Reagan (from left: Maynard Glitman, Max Kampelman, Reagan, Ronald Lehman, White House Chief of Staff Howard Baker), March 6, 1987

Enjoying a light moment in the Oval Office during the Washington summit, December 10, 1987

1988 summit in Moscow to sign the ICBM-reduction treaty. Reagan was pleased, especially because Gorbachev's letter did not appear to make the summit or the treaty signing contingent on eliminating the SDI program.

This third summit meeting reestablished the cautious but congenial relationship between Reagan and Gorbachev that had been nurtured at Geneva and tested severely at Reykjavik. Reagan mused: "I don't think the [INF] agreement would have been possible without our defense buildup. I also don't think it would have been possible before Gorbachev. He's quite a fellow. He's not above trying to bamboozle you as he tried to do to us at Reykjavik . . . but I believe he is a reasonable man. He is, as Margaret Thatcher once said, a man we can do business with."

The Washington Summit was an unqualified success: The INF Treaty was signed, the 1988 Moscow Summit was announced, as was the beginning of the more comprehensive strategic arms limitation treaty (START) talks that would lead to a Moscow signing the following year, Reagan's last year in office. In his remarks at the signing ceremony, Reagan emphasized the importance of adequate treaty-verification procedures to ensure that both nations keep their word.

REAGAN: We have listened to the wisdom in an old Russian maxim. And I'm sure you're familiar with it, Mr. General Secretary. The maxim is . . . "trust, but verify."

GORBACHEV: You repeat that at every meeting.

REAGAN: I like it.

Gorbachev and Reagan sign the INF Treaty to begin the arms reduction process, December 8, 1987

STATE OF THE UNION, 1988

*I thought the state of the union was pretty good that
night and said so before a joint session of Congress: The
country was strong, our economy prosperous, our spirits high.*

—RONALD REAGAN, *AN AMERICAN LIFE*

O N JANUARY 25, 1988, President Reagan delivered his eighth and final State of the Union address. He reminded his audience that government must always be kept under control by the people, and pointed to a five-foot-high stack of documents—the federal budget—next to him as proof of how difficult that could be. He quoted the ancient Chinese philosopher Lao-tzu ("Govern a great nation as you would cook a small fish: Don't overdo it.") and he expressed the hope that before his term was over the START agreement would be completed with the Soviet Union, so that actual reduction of nuclear warheads could begin. (Further progress was made that year, but it was for his successor, George Bush, to sign the agreement.)

*President Reagan discussing budget data for his State of the Union address with
Office of Management & Budget Director James Miller*

To illustrate just how mammoth government had become, Reagan used the Congress's Budget Reconciliation Act to highlight his speech in the well of the House of Representatives

THE LAST SUMMIT, MOSCOW, 1988

We were walking down the street in Moscow and, as a group of people recognized us from across the street, they began chanting, "USA, USA, USA" and "Free enterprise, free enterprise."

—RONALD REAGAN, COMMENTING IN HIS RETURN VISIT TO MOSCOW IN SEPTEMBER 1990, NEARLY TWO-AND-A-HALF YEARS AFTER HIS SUMMIT MEETING THERE

THE GLASNOST GENIE HAD been out of the bottle for three years when Ronald Reagan flew to Moscow for his final summit meeting as president. He had hoped to sign the Strategic Arms Reduction Treaty (START) with Soviet President Mikhail Gorbachev, but a number of details was still unresolved when the Reagans arrived in Moscow on May 29, 1988.

There were many positive signs in the U.S.–USSR relationship, just the same. At their previous summit, in Washington, in October 1987, Gorbachev had dropped his demand that the U.S. accept limitations on the Strategic Defense Initiative (SDI) as a prerequisite to signing an Intermediate Nuclear Forces (INF) treaty. The U.S. Senate ratified the INF treaty as the Reagans were traveling to Moscow and the president and Gorbachev signed it at the climax of the visit.

At their first meeting in Moscow, Gorbachev spoke of his desire for expanded trade with the United States. Reagan used this opening to note that Congress would be reluctant to do this in light of what were considered human rights abuses in the Soviet Union. The two leaders had a wide-ranging and, by their accounts, noncontentious, even cordial, series of meetings.

Taking advantage of the new openness in Soviet society, Reagan invited several dozen Soviet dissidents, human rights advocates, and intellectuals to the U.S. Embassy for a roundtable discussion and reception.

Yet, what was to become the most significant event of the visit—portending the great changes in Soviet society soon to come—was Reagan's speech to the students at Moscow State University.

Meeting with Gorbachev shortly after arriving in Moscow, May 29, 1988

There, under a huge bust of Lenin, the fortieth American president gave a remarkable speech about the possibilities of human invention, productivity, and wealth that can be unleashed under freedom and democracy. He said things that would not have been allowed to have been said in the Soviet Union only a few years before:

We Americans make no secret of our belief in freedom. In fact, it's something of a national pastime . . . Freedom is the right to question and

change the established way of doing things. It is the continuing revolution of the marketplace. It is the understanding that allows us to recognize shortcomings and seek solutions. It is the right to set forth an idea, scoffed at by the experts, and watch it catch fire among the people. It is the right to dream—to follow your dream or stick to your conscience, even if you're the only one in a sea of doubters.

Freedom is the recognition that no

single person, no single authority or government has a monopoly on the truth, but that every individual life is infinitely precious, that every one of us put on this world has been put there for a reason and has something to offer.

Commenting on this meeting with the students two years later, Reagan said, "There was simultaneous translation, so I soon realized that what they were applauding most were my references to freedom."

Schoolchildren welcome Nancy Reagan

ABOVE *The Reagans meet the people on Arbat Street*

LEFT *Freedom rings— beneath the bust of Lenin, Moscow State University, May 31, 1988*

RIGHT *The two leaders shake hands after signing the INF treaty, June 1, 1988*

UP FROM DEPENDENCY

Many people today are economically trapped in welfare. They'd like nothing better than to be out in the work-a-day world with the rest of us. Independence and self-sufficiency is what they want.

—RONALD REAGAN, REMARKS TO THE
NATIONAL ALLIANCE OF BUSINESS, OCTOBER 3, 1981

RONALD REAGAN HAD MADE welfare reform a major initiative of his second term as governor of California, and he addressed it again in his second term as president. He had long been critical of the outcome of Lyndon Johnson's War on Poverty, which had created a vast bureaucracy with a vested interest in keeping "clients" on welfare and had the effect of promoting single-parent families. In his 1986 State of the Union address he declared that the goal of welfare should be "real and lasting emancipation, because the success of welfare should be judged by how many of its recipients become independent of welfare." He directed his Domestic Policy Council to evaluate current welfare practices and develop a strategy to reduce dependency.

Ten months later, the council delivered to him a six-volume report title, *Up from Dependency*. It was a comprehensive analysis of the costly, cumbersome array of federal welfare programs then in existence. It recommended a new national strategy; a long-range reform process that would replace welfare with work, encourage the formation of two-parent families, and empower the states to tailor the new work-oriented welfare system to their specific needs. He announced the strategy in his next State of the Union address in 1987, and called on Congress to endorse it with legislation.

Reagan's welfare reform advisors were a diverse group, including former welfare recipients such as Kimi Gray, the national leader of the public housing resident management movement; Carol Sasaki, president of HOME (Helping Ourselves Means Education), a nationwide self-help

monitoring group of welfare "graduates"; and state governors such as Wisconsin's Tommy Thompson and New Jersey's Tom Kean, who had developed their own dependency-reduction reforms. All agreed the old system had to be scrapped and replaced by forms of public assistance that encouraged work and intact families.

Sharp divisions of opinion in Congress slowed development of the legislation Reagan sought. This led him, in July 1987, to create his own Low Income Opportunity Board to encourage state reforms and facilitate federal waivers for experimental programs. Wisconsin and New Jersey were the first two states to obtain waivers through the board. By the

The president's welfare reform experts meet, January 1987

time Reagan left office, eleven other states had received waivers, and twelve more had submitted requests.

Congress, meanwhile, finally reached consensus, and led by Sen. Daniel Patrick Moynihan of New York (and with strong pressure from the governors and the White House), passed in October 1988 the Family Support Act. This required the states to provide assistance to needy two-parent families and to set up extensive work and work-preparation programs. The act also established—for the first time—a federal requirement that welfare recipients work for their benefits. Although it was far more complicated than Reagan had wanted, and contained many work-avoidance loopholes, the Family Support Act nonetheless changed the basic thrust of welfare law and policy. Reagan signed it into law, hoping that he had set in motion a reform process that would eventually unravel America's welfare state.

ABOVE *The Family Support Act is signed* *(October 13, 1988)*

RIGHT *Reagan greets Kimi Gray, leader of the public housing resident management movement*

BELOW *Meeting in the White House with the Council for the Black Economic Agenda, led by Bob Woodson, to Reagan's left (February 1987)*

STEP ONE TO A NORTH AMERICAN FREE TRADE AGREEMENT

I, for one, am confident that we can show the world by example that the nations of North America are ready, within the context of an unswerving commitment to freedom, to seek new forms of accommodation to meet a changing world.

—RONALD REAGAN, IN AN ADDRESS ANNOUNCING HIS
1980 PRESIDENTIAL CANDIDACY, NEW YORK, NOVEMBER 13, 1979

RONALD REAGAN THUS opened his 1980 election campaign with a call for closer trade relations between the United States, Canada, and Mexico. He called it a "North American Accord." It would serve, he said, to spur economic growth and for the three countries of North America to coordinate aid to economically depressed nations in Central and South America. His larger goal was to strengthen the Western Hemisphere against further communist expansion without putting the United States in the despised role—to Latin Americans—of "The Great Colossus of the North."

On becoming president, Reagan's first trip outside the United States was to Ottawa, Canada, to get acquainted with Prime Minister Pierre Trudeau. Trudeau and, later, Mexican President José Lopez Portillo concurred with Reagan's vision of freer trade in North America and fraternal—not paternal—aid to Latin America. Reagan's message was: "We'll help you do the things you need to do,

but we won't come in and try to do them for you."

Implementation of this policy was slow in coming. Other, more pressing issues (such as how to stop communist military takeovers in Central America) sidetracked hemispheric trade initiatives. Also, Reagan frequently found himself at odds with Trudeau's socialist policies in Canada. As Reagan's policies began to pull the United States out of recession, Trudeau's government continued down the road of increased government ownership and economic control, stifling a recovery that should have kept pace with our own.

By 1984, Canada's voters turned Trudeau's party out and brought Brian Mulroney and his Progressive Conservative party to power. In moves Reagan applauded, Mulroney reversed a number of Trudeau's policies, established an economic revitalization program that encouraged foreign investment and privatization, and pulled Canada out of its recession. Mulroney quickly became a Reagan ally among foreign leaders.

In addition to his politics, Mulroney shared two other important qualities with Reagan: his Irish ancestry and his wit. Reagan remembered that during dinner at the Bonn, Germany, economic summit in 1985: "Instead of business, we got into storytelling, Brian Mulroney started it and I got on with some and a good time was had by all."

The upshot of the Reagan-Mulroney relationship was completion of the first step in what was to become the North American Free Trade Agreement: the U.S.–Canada Free Trade Agreement of 1988. It created what was then the largest free trade zone in the world. This led to the NAFTA, negotiated by Reagan's successor George Bush in 1992, and ratified by Congress in 1993.

OPPOSITE:

ABOVE *Signing the U.S.-Canada Free Trade Agreement, September 28, 1988*

BELOW *Lunch with the Mulroneys*

A FAREWELL TO GORBACHEV

*Gorbachev sounded as if he saw us as partners making a
better world.*

—RONALD REAGAN, *AN AMERICAN LIFE*

R ONALD REAGAN'S LAST
meeting, as president, with Mikhail
Gorbachev was in New York, only a
month and a half before Reagan was to
leave office. The Soviet leader came to
New York in December 1988 to tell the
United Nations that the Warsaw Pact
nations would be making major cuts in
their conventional forces.

Reagan took the opportunity to invite
Gorbachev to meet with him and
President-elect George Bush on
Governors' Island in New York harbor.
First the American leaders met privately
with him, then later joined officials of
both countries for lunch. It was a
sentimental journey in some respects for
both Reagan and Gorbachev. As they said
their farewells on the dock, both recalled
that they—and the world—had come a
long way since that day in Geneva in 1985
when the two men warily began their first
meeting. In that warm good-by neither
could foretell that soon the Soviet Union
itself would be history and within less than
three years Gorbachev himself would be
out of office.

*President Reagan gave a copy of this
photo to Mikhail Gorbachev at their New
York meeting. Its inscription: "We have
walked a long way together to clear a
path for peace. Geneva 1985—New York
1988"*

Presidents Gorbachev and Reagan and President-elect Bush, Governors' Island, New York, December 1988

A warm farewell to the Soviet leader on the dock at Governors' Island

OLD ENOUGH FOR GOLF

Fore!

—RONALD REAGAN, ABOUT TO TAKE A MOCK SWING
IN THE OVAL OFFICE

RONALD REAGAN WAS ONE OF the healthiest and physically best conditioned presidents in history. Being the oldest man ever elected to the office, he wore his good health as a badge of honor and physical competence. In 1987 he declared, "Since I came to the White House, I've gotten two hearing aids, had a colon operation, a prostate operation, skin cancer, and I've been shot . . . damn thing is, I never felt better."

By nature strong and active, Reagan also worked at being healthy. He didn't smoke, drank sparingly, took vitamin supplements, and had given up coffee with caffeine long before he became president. He preferred outdoor exercise, especially horseback riding, but regularly worked out indoors with exercise machines, treadmills, and weights. Recovering from the Hinckley assassination attempt in 1981, he worked out so assiduously in the White House exercise room that his chest expanded a full size and he had to buy new suits.

As a young man Reagan had been a better-than-average athlete—a strong swimmer and an ardent football player in high school and college. As he grew older swimming and football gave way to horseback riding and, on occasion, golf, a game played by many of his friends in Hollywood.

Several presidents have been avid golfers, most notably Dwight Eisenhower and Gerald Ford and, more recently, George Bush and Bill Clinton. Reagan, however, found that as president he had little time for golf, and played only one or

two rounds a year. His only regular golf date was on New Year's Eve at the private course of Walter Annenberg in Palm Springs, California.

One of Reagan's infrequent golf opportunities—a weekend at Augusta (Georgia) National Golf Course with Secretary of State George Shultz in October 1983—underscored the difficulty of mixing golf and the presidency. Arriving at Augusta with Nancy on Friday night, Reagan was awakened at 4:00 A.M. Saturday with news that the Organization of Eastern Caribbean States had requested U.S. military intervention in the Grenada revolution. After extensive discussions with his aides, he ordered the Grenada invasion, then headed for the golf course. He reasoned that to cancel the game might alert the news media and compromise the secrecy of the invasion.

In the middle of the game Secret Service agents rushed the president off the course and into a White House limousine, where he learned an armed man had invaded the golf course shop and taken hostages, including two White House aides. The man eventually released his hostages and gave himself up, but there was no more golf that day. The next morning, Sunday, Reagan was awakened at 2:30 with the news of the Beirut Marine barracks massacre. So much for the Sunday golf game. At 6:30 A.M., the Reagans boarded Air Force One to return to Washington.

When Reagan left the presidency and resumed life in Southern California, he looked forward to more leisure time and even signed up for golf lessons. Nearing eighty, he decided he was now "old enough to learn how to play golf."

OPPOSITE *Taking a full swing at his annual golfing weekend in Palm Springs, January 2, 1988*

ABOVE RIGHT *The president applies body english to a putt in the Oval Office with professional golf ace Raymond Floyd looking on*

BELOW RIGHT *New Year's Eve, 1988, at Palm Springs (left to right): Secretary of State George Shultz, golf pro Tom Watson, Reagan, pro Lee Trevino, host Walter Annenberg*

PASSING THE TORCH

We're about to enter the nineties, and some things have changed. Younger parents aren't sure that an unambivalent appreciation of America is the right thing to teach modern children. And, as for those who create the popular culture, well-grounded patriotism is no longer the style. Our spirit is back, but we haven't re-institutionalized it. We've got to do a better job of getting across that America is freedom—freedom of speech, freedom of religion, freedom of enterprise. And freedom is special and rare. It's fragile; it needs protection.

—RONALD REAGAN, FAREWELL ADDRESS FROM THE OVAL OFFICE, JANUARY 11, 1989

BY ALMOST ANY MEASURE, Ronald Reagan left the presidency and the nation better off than he found them. His economic policies pulled the nation out of the Carter recession and into the longest peacetime period of economic growth in history. His defense and foreign policies restored the United States to a position of international preeminence and brought the Soviet Union to the point of collapse. As Margaret Thatcher put it: "Ronald Reagan won the Cold War—without firing a shot."

Through his immense personal popularity and a leadership style based on adherence to principle, buoyant optimism, and a self-deprecating sense of humor, Reagan also achieved a consistency of presidential strength and influence achieved by few of his predecessors. Except for a few months during the Iran-Contra affair, when he grudgingly kept quiet during the deliberations of the Tower Commission, Reagan clearly dominated the national political scene, even though his party controlled only one house of Congress, from 1981 to 1987, and neither house during his last two years in office.

Reagan passed the torch to George Bush on January 20, 1989. Bush had won a landslide victory in November 1988 by reaffirming Reagan's policies, and Reagan had every reason to believe Bush would fulfill some of the goals Reagan had not achieved, especially a constitutional amendment to balance the budget and presidential line-item veto power to cut unnecessary spending.

On his last morning in office, Reagan received a final national security briefing from General Colin Powell, whom Bush would later appoint chairman of the Joint Chiefs of Staff. Powell's briefing was succinct and gratifying: "Mr. President," he said, "the world is quiet today."

The Reagans escorted George and Barbara Bush to the Capitol where, at noon, Bush was inaugurated as the forty-first President of the United States. From there, the Reagans boarded a helicopter to Andrews Air Force Base and their last ride on Air Force One. On the flight west to California, all those on board—staff members and the press—came by to shake hands and say goodbye. Champagne was poured and one of the group raised a glass with the toast, "Mission accomplished, Mr. President, mission accomplished."

BELOW LEFT *General Colin Powell, national security advisor, gives the president his daily briefing (New Year's Eve, Palm Springs, California, December 1988)*

BELOW RIGHT *Farewell reception with staff, January 18, 1989*

A HOME FOR THE
REAGAN LEGACY

Thirty-two years ago, when I was in Moscow . . . Nikita Khrushchev jabbed a finger into my chest and said, "Your grandchildren will live under communism." I responded, "Your grandchildren will live in freedom." At that time, I was sure he was wrong, but I was not sure I was right. And now we know—thanks in great part to the strong, idealistic leadership of President Ronald Reagan— Khruschev's grandchildren now live in freedom.

—FORMER PRESIDENT RICHARD NIXON, AT THE DEDICATION
OF THE REAGAN LIBRARY, SIMI VALLY, CALIFORNIA, NOVEMBER 4, 1991

THE RONALD REAGAN PRESIdential Library opened eleven years to the day after Reagan was elected president and thirty-four months after the end of his presidency. Much had happened since he left the White House. The Communist government of the Soviet Union had collapsed, and its constituent "republics" and satellites were struggling toward democratic capitalism while the West celebrated the end of the Cold War. Using the military muscle that had been restored by Reagan, the United States, in Desert Storm, had liberated Kuwait from the occupying armies of Saddam Hussein. The United States stood preeminent, the most powerful and influential nation on earth.

The Reagan Library, a 153,000-square-foot facility atop a high hill overlooking Simi Valley, California—halfway between Los Angeles and Santa Barbara—was built to house Reagan's presidential records and personal papers, in accordance with the federal Presidential Records Act. Both the land and the building had been paid for with privately donated funds, the facility to be operated by the National Archives.

The opening drew many celebrities from the worlds of politics, entertainment, and business, but most of the attention was focused on the fact that, for the first time in the nation's history, five presidents were gathered in one place. Reagan's three immediate predecessors—

Richard Nixon, Gerald Ford, and Jimmy Carter—together with his successor— George Bush—had come together to honor both Reagan and the presidency. The wives of all five were there, as were Lyndon Johnson's widow, Lady Bird, and John Kennedy's son and daughter.

Dr. Ralph Bledsoe, director of the Reagan Library, gave the five presidents a guided tour of the facility, then led them to the outdoor dais for the opening ceremonies. Charlton Heston, a longtime friend of the Reagans and an actor who had played kings and even God, was master of ceremonies. The weather was warm and the sky clear, but with a snapping breeze that blew the flags straight out from their poles. Heston pointed out to the crowd how pleasant the weather was, then in a resonant god-like voice, acknowledged the applause with, "You're welcome." He apologized for the breeze as "something that just slipped My mind."

California Governor Pete Wilson introduced the several presidents and each spoke briefly. All praised Reagan, none more fully than Jimmy Carter, the sole Democrat among them. But it was Richard Nixon who put Reagan's presidency into historical perspective, praising him as "one who had profound beliefs, who had the courage to fight for those beliefs, and who had the eloquence to inspire his fellow Americans to support those beliefs."

Then it was Reagan's turn. As he walked to the microphone, in an eerie reprise of the clouds parting at his first presidential Inaugural, the distracting breeze for which Heston had humorously apologized suddenly died. The flags hung limp and the weather went from good to perfect.

Reagan praised his fellow presidents and their wives, his parents and Nancy, and the heroes who had sustained America in difficult times. He spoke from the vantage point of age:

Eighty years is a long time to live. And yet, within the course of only a few short years, I have seen the world turned upside down and conventional wisdom utterly disproved.

Visitors to this mountaintop will see a great jagged chunk of that Berlin Wall—hated symbol of, yes, an evil empire that spied on and lied to its citizens, denying them their freedom, their bread, even their faith. Well, today, that wall exists only in museums, souvenir collections, and memories of people no longer oppressed.

He spoke also from the optimism he had inherited and the sense of humor he had nurtured:

The Ronald Reagan Presidential Library

I have been described as an undying optimist, always seeing the glass half full when some see it as half empty. And, yes, it's true. I always see the sunny side of life. And that's not just because I've been blessed by achieving so many of my dreams. My optimism comes not just from my strong faith in God, but from my strong and enduring faith in man.

In my 80 years—I prefer to call that the 41st anniversary of my 39th birthday—I've seen what men can do for each other and to each other. I've seen war and peace, feast and famine, depression and prosperity, sickness and health. I've seen the depth of suffering and the peaks of triumph. And I know in my heart that man is good; that what is right will always eventually triumph; and that there is purpose and worth to each and every life.

And, he concluded with . . .

Proverbially, old men plant trees, even though they do not expect to see their fruition. So it is with presidents. The doors of this library are open now and all are welcome. The judgment of history is left to you, the people.

I have no fears of that, for we have done our best. And so I say, come and learn from it. My fondest hope is that Americans will travel the road extending forward from the arch of experience, never forgetting our heroic origins, never failing to seek

Divine guidance as we march boldly, bravely into a future limited only by our capacity to dream.

May every day be a new beginning and every dawn bring us closer to that shining city on the hill.

Five presidents inspect the INF treaty display

Presidents Bush, Reagan, Carter, Ford, and Nixon in front of the library

Five presidents, six first ladies

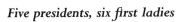

The sun sets on a fragment of the Berlin Wall outside the Reagan Library

PHOTOGRAPHERS' CREDITS

White House photographers are identified by last name; "Unid." signifies that the Archives' contact print sheet from which the photograph was selected did not identify the photographer. For pages with more than one photograph, credits are assigned clockwise, starting with the photograph closest to the upper left-hand corner of the page.

PAGE	PHOTOGRAPHER(S)
13	Unid.
16	Evans
17	Fitz-Patrick
18, 19	Unid.
20	Knightlinger, Knightlinger, Brown
21	Evans
22	Evans
23	Unid., Knightlinger
24	Evans
25	Evans, Schumacher, Evans
26	Evans
27	Evans, Schumacher
28	Schumacher, Souza
29	Evans, Souza
30	Unid.
32	Souza
33	Souza
34	Fackelman-Miner
35	Knightlinger, Evans, Evans, Evans
36	Evans
37	Unid.
38	Arthur
39	Souza, Fackelman-Miner
40	Unid.
41	Unid., Fackelman-Minor, Unid.
42	Unid.
43	Evans
44	Fitz-Patrick, Fitz-Patrick
45	Fitz-Patrick, Unid.
47	Fackelman-Miner, Fackelman-Miner
49	Evans, Unid.
50	Evans, Unid.
51	Arthur, Fitz-Patrick
52	Evans, Harrity (*U.S. News*, Library of Congress Collection)
53	Fitz-Patrick
54	Unid., Fitz-Patrick
55	Fitz-Patrick
56	Knightlinger
57	Unid.
58	Fackelman-Miner, Fitz-Patrick
59	Biddle, Unid.
60	Knightlinger
61	Evans, Evans, Evans

PAGE	PHOTOGRAPHER(S)
62	Knightlinger
64	Souza, Unid.
65	Fitz-Patrick, Unid., Biddle
66	Evans
67	Biddle, Unid.
68	Evans
69	Souza, Evans
70	Unid.
71	Unid., Souza
72	Unid.
73	Souza, Unid.
74	Fitz-Patrick
75	Fitz-Patrick, Evans
76	Schumacher
77	Knightlinger, Fitz-Patrick
78	Fitz-Patrick
79	Souza
80	Fackelman-Miner
81	Souza, Fackelman-Miner
82	Souza, Fackelman-Miner, Biddle
83	Souza, Fackelman-Miner
84	Fitz-Patrick
85	Knightlinger, Fitz-Patrick
86	Unid.
87	Fackelman-Miner, Unid.
89	Evans, Evans
90	Souza
91	Knightlinger
92	Evans
93	Unid.
94	Souza
95	Souza
96	Evans
97	Fitz-Patrick, Souza
98	Unid.
99	Souza, Evans
100	Knightlinger
101	Unid.
102	Unid., Souza, Evans
103	Souza, Evans, Unid.
104	Souza
105	Unid., Fackelman-Miner
106	Souza, Unid.
107	Unid.

PAGE	PHOTOGRAPHER(S)
108	Unid.
109	Unid.
110	Unid.
111	Fitz-Patrick, Souza
112	Unid.
113	Unid.
114	Unid.
115	Unid., Fitz-Patrick
116	Fitz-Patrick
117	Fitz-Patrick, Souza
118	Fitz-Patrick
119	Fackelman-Miner, Fackelman-Miner, Fitz-Patrick
120	Unid.
121	Arthur, Arthur
122	Souza
123	Fackelman-Miner, Fackelman-Miner
125	Fitz-Patrick, Souza, Arthur
126	Souza
127	Souza, Fitz-Patrick
128	Souza
129	Arthur, Souza
130	Souza, Arthur
131	Souza
132	Souza
133	Unid., Souza
134	Dean
135	Fitz-Patrick, Arthur, Unid.
136	Fernald
137	Fackelman-Miner, Fitz-Patrick, Souza
138	Souza
139	Biddle
140	Dean
141	Biddle, Souza, Fitz-Patrick, Fitz-Patrick
142	Fackelman-Miner
143	Unid., Unid., Arthur
145	Biddle, Fitz-Patrick
146	Arthur
147	Unid.
148	Biddle
149	Unid., Souza
150	Souza, Souza
151	Souza (with Bush), Biddle (Oval Office)
153–155	Reagan Library